PET LOSS

PET LOSS

A THOUGHTFUL GUIDE FOR ADULTS AND CHILDREN

HERBERT A. NIEBURG
AND
ARLENE FISCHER

 HarperPerennial
A Division of HarperCollins*Publishers*

The Library of Congress has catalogued the hardcover edition as follows:

Nieburg, Herbert A.
    Pet loss.
    Bibliography: p.
    Includes index.
    ISBN 0-06-014947-7
    1. Children and animals. 2. Pet owners—Psychology. 3. Bereavement—
Psychological aspects. I. Fischer, Arlene. II. Title
BF723.A45N53
155.9'37   81-47670

ISBN 0-06-092678-3 (pbk.)

05 04 03 02 01 RRD 10 9 8 7 6 5

To Lise and Bruno
and
To Robert, Stephen and Elizabeth Fischer.
And Ginger, too.

Contents

Acknowledgments

A special thanks to our editor, Lawrence Peel Ashmead, for his encouragement, availability and excellent editorial guidance. And to Wendy Sclight, a "wordsmith wonder," for her advice.

Thanks also to the others who contributed their expertise and insight to the preparation of this book: Jack Anteleyes, D.V.M., Joan Baron, Peter Borchelt, Ph.D., Roger Caras, Stephen D. Fischer, Carole Fudin, C.S.W., James Harris, D.V.M., Roger Harris, Linda Jacobson, D.V.M., Aaron Katcher, M.D., William J. Kay, D.V.M., Judy Kimberg, Roger Kindler, Esq., A. Christine MacMurray, Lise B. Mayers, Craig Nelson, Ellen Popper, Betty Rosenzweig, Donald C. Sawyer, D.V.M., Ph.D., Alan Schreier, V.M.D., Peter Bentley Scolnik, Fredda R. Tourin, Joan Weiner, and Carl Wiedemann, Ph.D. And to the kind people who shared their pet-related experiences with us.

—*Herbert Nieburg and Arlene Fischer*

Foreword

If you ever love an animal, there are three days in your life you will always remember.

The first is a day, blessed with happiness, when you bring home your young new friend.

You may have spent weeks deciding on a breed. You may have asked numerous opinions of many vets, or done long research in finding a breeder. Or, perhaps in a fleeting moment, you may have just chosen that silly looking mutt in a shelter—simply because something in its eyes reached your heart.

But when you bring that chosen pet home, and watch it explore, and claim its special place in your hall or frontroom—and when you feel it brush against you for the first time—it instills a feeling of pure love you will carry with you through the many years to come.

The second day will occur eight or nine or ten years later.

It will be a day like any other. Routine and unexceptional. But, for a surprising instant, you will look at your longtime friend and see age where you once saw youth.

You will see slow deliberate steps where you once saw energy.

And you will see sleep where you once saw activity.

So you will begin to adjust your friend's diet—and you may add a pill or two to her food.

And you may feel a growing fear deep within yourself, which bodes of a coming emptiness.

And you will feel this uneasy feeling, on and off, until the third day finally arrives.

And on this day—if your friend and God have not decided for you, then you will be faced with making a decision of your own—on behalf of your lifelong friend, and with the guidance of your own deepest Spirit.

But whichever way your friend eventually leaves you—you will feel as alone as a single star in the dark night sky.

If you are wise, you will let the tears flow as freely and as often as they must. And if you are typical, you will find that not many in your circle of family or human friends will be able to understand your grief, or comfort you.

But if you are true to the love of the pet you cherished through the many joyfilled years, you may find that a soul—a bit smaller in size than your own—seems to walk with you, at times, during the lonely days to come.

And at moments when you least expect anything out of the ordinary to happen, you may feel something brush against your leg——very very lightly.

And looking down at the place where your dear, perhaps dearest, friend used to lay—you will remember those three significant days.

The memory will most likely be painful, and leave an ache in your heart——

As time passes the ache will come and go as if it has a life of its own.

You will both reject it and embrace it, and it may confuse you.

If you reject it, it will depress you.

If you embrace it, it will deepen you.

Either way, it will still be an ache.

But there will be, I assure you, a fourth day when—along

with the memory of your pet—and piercing through the heaviness in your heart—there will come a realization that belongs only to you.

It will be as unique and strong as our relationship with each animal we have loved, and lost.

This realization takes the form of a Living Love——

Like the heavenly scent of a rose that remains after the petals have wilted, this Love will remain and grow—and be there for us to remember.

It is a Love we have earned.

It is the legacy our pets leave us when they go——

And it is a gift we may keep with us as long as we live.

It is a Love which is ours alone——

And until we ourselves leave, perhaps to join our Beloved Pets——

It is a Love that we will always possess.

—Martin Scot Kosins

Introduction

This book belongs to all of us who have ever loved a pet. In our society we are expected to underplay our sorrow over the death of a cat or dog, but the truth is that our feelings often linger on, long after the loss has taken place. While the impact may not be the same as occurs with human loss, the reactions can be intense enough to cause strong emotional and even physical disturbances. After all, our pets have shared our lives, our homes and our affection.

How do we manage to deal with this distress? The sensible answer is that we allow ourselves to mourn—to explore our attachment and admit our sense of loss, to accept our stress and treat it openly. The complication is that we don't want to. We feel embarrassed owning up to grief over the death of an animal. For in our culture, there really is no acceptable way of mourning a pet.

In his practice as a grief therapist, Herbert Nieburg recognized the ache that pet loss can trigger in many people and the tendency to suppress it. He also recognized that such repression of grief had an adverse effect on his clients' well-being. By not dealing with their feelings, they were allowing the pain to remain unrelieved, like an untended sore that never quite heals and interferes with normal functioning. He discovered that when pet loss is repressed in childhood—by parents, for example, who minimize their youngsters' feelings over a cat or dog—it often comes back to haunt the adult. Unreleased grief stays with us. When we suffer a later loss, all of the pain we held down rises to the surface. We are, in effect, carrying a double load, mourning both the present and the past loss.

Traditional attitudes of society may well contribute to making us ashamed to mourn our companion animals. Under the laws of most states, pets are still considered merely items of personal property rather than objects of affection with a value beyond a market appraisal. From that perspective, how can grieving be justified for dogs or cats?

Yet human-pet attachment has existed for centuries. The kinship between dogs and humans dates back at least 10,500 years according to researchers who studied the remains of prehistoric camps—when wild dogs provided protection to the caveman in exchange for a share of the hunt. The kinship with cats developed somewhat later. Felines were domesticated about 5,000 years ago by the Egyptians, who were impressed with their ability to exterminate rats and mice as well as their aloof and mysterious natures. And the relationship has been thriving ever since. Today, in the United States alone, there are 48 million pet dogs and 27.2 million pet cats living in 45 million households. That is well over half (58 percent) of the homes in this country.

Why is it, then, if the human-pet connection has existed for thousands of years, the subject of pet loss is only now being recognized and explored? Perhaps it is because mental health professionals and medical investigators are beginning to study human-pet relationships and discover the value of pets to human beings.

In his book *Pets and Human Development*, the psychologist Boris Levinson suggests that pets can help human beings from infancy to old age solve developmental problems by providing affection, instilling a sense of competence through the experience of nurturing and by relieving loneliness. He also suggests that dogs and cats can be used in psychological evaluation and in work with physically handicapped children.

Some specialists have recommended that certain of their patients with psychiatric disorders acquire pets upon discharge from the hospital as one means of becoming reintegrated into the outside world. There has also been clinical evidence, reported in *Public Health Reports* (July–August, 1980) that pet ownership can add significantly to the probability of survival in heart-attack patients after discharge from a coronary-care unit—although the reason for this has not been determined.

We live for the most part in a high-pressure world. Pets soften that world by giving us pleasure, recreation and uncritical affection, without seeking much in return. Our human relationships are often a great deal more complicated and demanding.

Of course, not every owner is affected equally by the death of a cat or dog. We know that pets mean different things to different people. But when the idea that people should let themselves grieve over the loss of their pets was discussed in *The New York Times,* in an article written by Arlene Fischer ("When a Pet's Death Hurts Its Master," May 8, 1980), the response was swift and surprisingly strong. Herbert Nieburg, who was interviewed in the article because of his published work in pet loss, received nearly two hundred requests for help with anticipated loss, actual loss, the euthanasia dilemma, children's reactions and other problems. Pet owners were obviously reaching out for reassurance and guidance on a matter of significance to them—and one about which very little had been written.

The purpose of this book is to provide such guidance and to offer insight into the many reasons for human–pet attachment and the painful reactions, both typical and unusual, that are brought about by loss.

Since children are deeply affected by the death of a cat or dog, there are detailed guidelines to help parents deal with their youngsters' questions and feelings. There is also practical advice on helping owners cope when the pet's death is accidental, ranging from what to do immediately following a severe or fatal injury to the legal recourse that is available when injury or death is caused by someone else's negligence.

The euthanasia dilemma is explored in depth, from the circumstances that can lead to this difficult decision to an evaluation of the various methods used.

An important decision, which many pet owners avoid in advance, concerns arrangements that must be made following a pet's death. There is discussion of the various services offered, including individual or communal burial or cremation and the relative costs and merits of each.

And, since replacement is one of the most effective ways of dealing with pet loss, we examine the signs that let people know when, or if, they are ready to have a new pet.

Sometimes people cannot keep their pets because of changes in their lives; or their animals may disappear. The effects of loss unrelated to death are explored with practical suggestions, ranging from locating a missing animal to finding a new home for a pet.

The role of the veterinarian is examined, with emphasis on the advice and support clients can expect from these professionals.

We also answer frequently asked questions that arise concerning anticipated or actual pet loss.

Perhaps the most important message this book can bring, however, is that with every attachment comes loss, and it is perfectly acceptable to grieve over that loss.

For the sake of continuity and style, the male gender is used throughout the book to denote both sexes, rather than the his/her construction.

When the body that lived at your single will,
With its whimper of welcome is stilled (how still!)
When the spirit that answered your every mood
Is gone—wherever it goes—for good,
You will discover how much you care,
And will give your heart to a dog to tear.

—RUDYARD KIPLING,
"The Power of the Dog"

PET LOSS

1 Pets as Objects of Affection

Just one week ago I lost my beloved St. Bernard, Rascal. He was only ten weeks old when I got him—as a surprise for my sixteenth birthday. For nine years he was a part of my life. Now it's very painful to come into the house and not find him here. His presence is everywhere. I don't believe I will ever get over the ache the loss has left in my heart.

—SUSAN L.

Anyone who ever loved a pet can understand the feelings of loss that follow the death of an animal companion.

When Rascal died, his young owner lost a friend. He had padded after her as a puppy and continued to be a part of her day-to-day life for years. They had their routines, responded to each other's moods. Now, when her key turns in the lock, instead of getting an excited greeting, Susan is met with silence. No wonder she is having difficulty dealing with the empty spaces left by Rascal's death.

The distress Susan feels is not at all uncommon—millions of people, of every age and background, have experienced or will undergo the stress of pet loss. To many owners, pets are like members of the family, with personalities of their own. Common sense tells us that because of the differences in relative life-spans in all likelihood we will lose our pets. Yet the loss of a lovingly raised cat or dog can take a slice out of one's life.

What makes it especially difficult is that often, despite their sense of attachment, people are disturbed by their feelings. Surely, they tell themselves, such strong grief is appropriate only for the loss of a human friend.

But in fact, grief is not a feeling that is reserved for the loss of friends or relatives. Grief is a normal reaction whenever we undergo an important loss of any kind, and the depth of the grief depends on the attachment we have to what is lost.

Psychologists explain attachment as a tie of affection to any significant object—even an inanimate one—that fills a particular need. A shredded baby blanket, for example, will help a toddler bridge the gap between infancy and the more demanding world of childhood. Removing it will cause the baby to respond with distress. And the teenage boy who lavishes care on his first car—the symbol of his coming of age—will suffer when it is damaged.

John Bowlby, a British psychiatrist who has studied attachments, found that any unwilling separation or loss of objects of attachment "gives rise to many forms of emotional distress and personality disturbance."

He found that symptoms of such distress include anger, loneliness and emptiness—and these are, not surprisingly, the very feelings that pet owners experience when their animals are suddenly gone.

Identifying Your Pet's Meaning to You

As with human losses, the first step in dealing with painful pet loss is to examine your attachments: what did your pet mean to you? It is important to identify these bonds for two reasons. Examining the connections that held you to your pet will help you accept the intensity of your reaction to the loss. And understanding what the attachments were based on will let you begin to seek other ways to satisfy the needs once met by your pet.

The attachments felt between pet owners and animals, of course, vary widely. Those who own animals for purely practical reasons—such as the restaurant owner who buys a cat to rid his place of rats and mice—are likely to accept the pet's death without great sorrow. Their animals filled important needs, but the emotional bonds may not have been particularly strong. At the other extreme are a small number of people who, perhaps because of the inability to form healthy relationships with other humans, have unreasonable attachments to their pets. These people frequently see their pets as extensions of themselves, and project their own attitudes and feelings onto the animal. Their pet's death may represent their own demise, or it may signal the end of their most meaningful relationship, and the grief reactions can be extreme and require professional help.

For many people, however, the pet attachment is strong without being overwhelming. The ties are often varied; some are more important than others. Among the things that pets provide are uncritical love, companionship, pride and self-esteem; also, they serve as substitute relatives, protectors, social assets, promoters of physical exercise, and reminders of other people, places or times. And the relationships change as we move through life: children rely on pets for unqualified acceptance, childless couples enjoy lavishing care and training on a pet, people who live alone love their pets for mutual companionship, and elderly persons may appreciate being needed in an otherwise "empty nest."

In the following pages, these differing types of attachments are described. More than one may apply to the relationship between owners and their pets, but understanding the reasons for the attachments, as varied and complex as they may be, is the first step in accepting and overcoming the grief that follows when the bond is severed.

Love with No Strings Attached

Probably the most meaningful quality that pets provide us with is unqualified love and acceptance. So often, human affection must be gained with a great deal of effort and sacrifice, but pets give us a readily available, seemingly endless supply of love and ask virtually nothing in return. If we leave our pets out in the rain, forget to feed them, or unfairly direct our anger at them, they forgive us. We do not have to impress our animal companions with our charm, intelligence or other agreeable qualities to earn their devotion. Their affection is extended without guile: there is no mistaking a thumping tail or a friendly rub; it signals "I'm glad to see you and I won't pretend I'm not."

Because they give us the love we crave, it is easy to understand our attachment. Sometimes, in fact, we may feel as though we love our cats or dogs too much, but if a pet provides a large measure of comfort, without lessening our relations with other human beings, there is nothing wrong with a strong tie.

A Constant Companion

It is hard to think of pets without immediately thinking of companionship. When we are lonely, we have an unfailing source to turn to. Exchanges of affection can take place in comfortable silence, giving us the opportunity for an easygoing relationship. Our pets will uncomplainingly keep us company in bed, alongside the bathtub, on a walk, in a truck, at the refrigerator at midnight or elsewhere, without requiring sparkling conversation to hold them there. By their very natures, pets are responsive to human moods and assuage our loneliness, respond to our playfulness, match our bursts of energy in perfect rhythm.

This type of attachment is often entwined with long-established routines and habits, which serve as sad reminders when the pet is no longer there to share them. We pause at the front door, waiting for the excited greeting; we glance at the window sill, recalling our cat's furry Buddha-like profile. It is hard on us when we lose these companions. We respond naturally with feelings of loneliness and emptiness and often with a lack of concentration on matters that normally take our attention. In a sense, we are searching for our lost companion.

The Pride of Ownership

The pets that share our lives also reinforce our own self-images. The free-spirited find joy in romping through the park with a footloose canine; children take special delight in the antics of puppies or kittens that mirror their own playful natures; disciplined people work with pride in training and showing their pets; the male with the macho image strides along with a dog as big as a horse; the woman with a strong maternal instinct finds it fulfilling to nurture her pet.

There is great satisfaction in overseeing the development of another living being, encouraging the traits you personally value. And the relationship between people and their new dependents often develops quickly. One moment the cat or dog is a stranger living with a breeder, at a pet store, or on the streets, and the next it has been adopted and swiftly accepted as the newest member of the family. Such instant bonding is understandable. Dogs and cats reach in and pull out our desire to care for another living being. For some people the first bonds are formed on the trip home with their pet; others become emotionally connected during the first walk or the first time the animal responds to training.

Even when people attempt to stave off emotional attachment to an animal, they often have difficulty remaining aloof. The following vignette is an example:

When Linda's father was sidelined from work with a fractured hip, he was becoming increasingly depressed. So Linda decided to surprise him with a Father's Day gift. She made arrangements to buy him a poodle puppy because he had owned several as a young boy and he considered them "his treasures." Linda recalls the day that she brought the puppy home:

Father was sitting in the backyard on a chaise lounge and I bent over and put the scruffy ball of fluff in his lap and I said "Happy Father's Day." He took one look at it and said, "What in the world is this?" And I said, "It's a poodle puppy. I know you love poodles." "It looks like a monkey," he said and he gave it back to me. I could tell that he did not want to become attached because eventually he would have to go back to work and he would miss Cognac.

It was really very amusing. The dog would come over to him and my father would turn his back, or try to turn his back. Well, that lasted for three days, and the next thing you know the dog was sitting in his lap and licking his face and lying on the bed with him and lying on his stomach on the couch. It didn't take long for him to be completely accepted by everybody. Cognac was the new baby in the family.

While the efforts required—the feedings, the walks no matter what weather, visits to the vet—may not be enjoyable, the chores serve to enhance the feelings of responsibility that often add to a person's self-esteem. This type of attachment can be quite powerful, for the pride of a well-cared-for pet is highly satisfying. When their pets die, owners may feel as if they have lost a part of themselves.

Substitute Relative

Kenneth M. G. Keddie, an English psychiatrist studying pathological grief over the death of pets, found that pets are often regarded by their owners not simply as companions, but also, in today's "inward-looking nuclear family," as "surrogate relatives." He observed pets taking on the roles of parent, sibling, spouse or offspring and providing a special supportive relationship. This may be seen in the following story:

Carl, a successful psychiatrist, lived with his wife and young daughter in Tennessee. When the little girl turned eight, the family decided to buy a dog to keep her company. As it turned out, Charlie became Carl's dog—the two were so close that Carl's wife teased him about finally getting the brother he had always wanted. It was rare to see Carl without the retriever at his side; the two jogged together each morning, Charlie kept Carl company when he worked at home and they often spent weekends camping and hiking in the mountains. One morning, as they were finishing their run, Charlie darted across the road after a rabbit and was struck by a car and killed instantly. As Carl struggled with his grief in the days following Charlie's death, he realized that his wife had been close to the truth: the dog had represented, to some extent, the companion brother he had always wished for as an only child. Because of his training as a psychiatrist, Carl was able to understand that he was mourning his "lost" relative and the end of an imaginary relationship, as well as his loved retriever.

A Protector

At a time when a rising crime rate makes us feel open to harm in our homes and on the streets, pets provide us with a large measure of physical and psychological protection. We walk outside in the dark, or sleep more comfortably knowing that our combination bodyguard/burglar alarm is alert to strangers. Some individuals acquire guard dogs because their specific living or working conditions require such trained animals. But the sounds from even the smallest dogs may be enough to warn an owner and to deter an intruder. When the animal that served us as a protector is gone, we feel uneasy and vulnerable.

A Social Asset

Pet owners often become, simply by virtue of owning a pet, part of a little clique or social group. Dog walkers, for example, may meet every day at the same time for some congenial conversation as their dogs romp. Often these are casual relationships that never go much beyond pleasantries and exchanging information about the pets; sometimes, though, ownership of a pet may provide the entree into a more lasting friendship.

As a case in point, Laurie, an inventive young woman, was able to use her dog as an effective ambassador when she moved to New York City from the Midwest. Living alone in an impersonal city made meeting people difficult. But her schnauzer, Fritzy, made friends with the other animals quite easily, so Laurie decided to capitalize on his popularity. She rented a local pet-grooming store on a Saturday afternoon and invited a number of dogwalkers with whom she had a nodding acquaintance to a birthday party for Fritzy. The neighborhood pets arrived in all their beribboned finery and it was a boisterous, good-natured affair—where Laurie was able to begin several lasting friendships.

For those whose attachment to a pet brings these kind of relationships with other people, losing the pet may make them feel closed out of an informal but satisfying "brother-hood."

The Great Outdoors

Many of us tend to resist physical activity unless we have a reason. Walking, jogging and playing with our pets gets us moving. The Austrian social behaviorist Konrad Lorenz, who worked extensively with animals, expresses the enjoyment he gets from walking with his own dog: "The pleasure I derive from my dog is closely akin to the joy accorded to me by the raven, greylag goose or other wild animals that enliven my walks through the countryside; it seems like a reestablishment of the immediate bond with that unconscious omniscience called nature."

When we lose a pet, we may give up our daily outings, and miss the sheer fun of playing with our animal. "Walking alone," said one former pet owner, "makes me feel incomplete."

A Reminder

An owner's attachment to a pet may not be based just on the animal's attributes, but may involve a bond with another person, place or time, which the pet has come to represent. The story of Janet is an example: The fifty-three-year-old woman was deeply depressed when her Siamese cat, Ming, died. Although she had great affection for him, she could not understand the degree of her reaction, because Ming did not actually belong to her. He had been purchased for her daughter when she was a teenager. Only after exploring the pet owner history with a therapist did the reason for the depression become apparent. Janet's daughter, a promising law student, had committed suicide six months before. For Janet, the pet was the last living vestige of her child. With the death of Ming, Janet's daughter was finally and irrevocably lost.

With this type of attachment, the pet's death triggers grief on two levels—the real and the symbolic. To successfully overcome the sorrow, the owner must deal with the loss of the animal and also the feelings about the object of attachment which the pet represented.

Attachments at Varying Stages of Life

Certain types of bonds are often found at certain stages of life, for people develop relationships with their pets to fulfill the needs they have at that time.

Childhood

A child often invests emotional energy in a dog or cat in order to obtain acceptance, security and reassurance from a temporarily unloving world. No matter what outrageous act the child has committed, no matter how flagrantly he or she has violated the rules set down by family, society, school or friends, the pet is there to provide uncritical love. When Johnny's cat or dog nudges open his door, jumps up on his bed and nuzzles his troubled young face, the message comes through: "Hey, you're not so bad. Somebody around here loves you." The pet's very presence reminds the youngster that something in his world is still worthwhile. (A full discussion of child-pet relationships can be found in Chapter 3.)

Childless Couples

For many childless couples, pets, not surprisingly, symbolize the progeny they do not have. Through a responsive dog or cat, the owners can assume responsibility and authority and lavish whatever amount of love and attention they are inclined to give. Many psychologists view this attachment as completely appropriate when a family is not desirable, practical or possible. Some owners, however, tend to invest the dog or cat with childlike needs and fears. Like other "parents," they are deeply concerned about their "baby's" welfare, and feel more comfortable when the pet accompanies them on all manner of outings, from shopping expeditions to weekends away.

Stories abound about startled hosts or hostesses finding a threesome at the front door when they expected only a pair of two-legged guests. And of insulted guests who departed in a huff because their "little one" wasn't welcome. In cases of such intense attachments, owners are loath to leave their pets in kennels and frequently cancel their plans rather than "abandon" their loved animals. This relationship can be deemed unhealthy if it interferes with daily functioning.

People who use their pets in place of children can expect to experience the same types of painful separation and grief responses that a parent goes through with the loss of a child.

Those Who Live Alone

Individuals living alone often rely on pets to stave off loneliness and help them participate in life. In fact, it is not at all unusual for single adults to own several animals. Perhaps, unconsciously, they are choosing a set of friends that will not disappoint, reject or otherwise hurt them. And through their animals, they often find ways of making contact with the outside world. Pets are figures to love and to care for, and they respond with attention and affection when there is no one else to give it.

Divorced or separated people often have strong attachments to the pets they lived with during marriage, particularly when they have no children. Caring for the dog or cat provides a continuity of routine and helps ease the transition from the old lifestyle to the new. Often, the animal represents one of the few memories of shared good times in the couple's crumbled relationship. The pet's loss at such a significant time can trigger painful feelings of abandonment.

In his book *Pets and Human Development*, the psychologist Boris M. Levinson has suggested that, for isolated individuals living on the fringes of society, "association with a pet may make the difference between maintaining contact with reality or almost totally withdrawing into fantasy. It may make the difference between life and death."

In cases where there are no significant companions other than the pet, the owner's grief reactions can be extreme. It is very important to have support from friends and family at this time. It is also advisable to replace the pet as soon as possible (see Chapter 7).

Older Adults

Many older adults who live increasingly sedentary and isolated existences find purpose in life through caring for pets. They may no longer feel needed by their grown children and are frequently bored or disappointed with retirement. Their circle of friends is likely to be decreasing through illness and death. In addition, the elderly often must depend on others for physical care. However, a loved pet to care for allows the owner to feel productive, to engage more actively in life and to establish a strong emotional tie. For older adults, especially those who are vigorous and healthy, being needed is an essential ingredient of self-respect. The following story is illustrative:

For years Ginny worked in the circulation department of a large newspaper. As her birthday approached, the sixty-four-year-old woman grumbled incessantly to her co-workers about her mandatory retirement, viewing it as "the beginning of the end, absolutely." Her husband, Jock, had retired two years earlier and had set a poor example: at times he was demanding and irritable, at other times, listless and apathetic. So Ginny regarded retirement as a series of dreary, empty days.

But on the day before she was due to retire, Ginny found an odd-shaped box on her desk. Inside was a little ball of white fur that stretched and purred and caught Ginny's finger in its paw. Ginny named the cat Pica, and within the month, she and Jock had visited a pet store and acquired a little striped Elite. The two cats played a substantial role in helping the couple set aside their resentment about retirement and begin enjoying their time at home.

From childhood to old age, we establish special relationships with our pets that fill a whole range of physical and emotional needs. The disruption of these attachments when our pets die brings about feelings of sorrow and distress. But by recognizing that our attachments are significant and enduring, and by understanding what they represent, we will be ready to take the first step toward working through the stress of pet loss.

2 Separation: Understanding Your Grief

When a beloved pet dies, some people simply accept the death as a natural part of life. Others, by virtue of their minimum attachment, are able to tolerate the separation without a great deal of pain. But people who have strong ties to their pets are often deeply affected by grief, which can temporarily overshadow other aspects of their lives.

Crying and feeling lonely or depressed are natural ways of responding to the death of a cat or dog that has shared one's daily life. There is a classic definition by grief therapist Colin Murray Parkes of grief as an emotional and behavioral reaction that is set in motion when a love tie is broken. A "love tie" accurately describes the relationship between many people and their pets: the loss deprives the owner of love as well as other basic needs and pleasures. Is it any wonder that such a good companion is sorely missed?

But some people expect ridicule from their friends or relatives if they talk about their sorrow. They don't dare risk crying or sharing their feelings except with other pet lovers. They are torn by the conflicting needs to behave in a socially acceptable way and to release their sorrow.

It seems weak and "immature" to give in to such emotions. One young woman wrote: "I learned two weeks ago that my eight-year-old cat was terminally ill, and by the weekend we had to turn to euthanasia. It was so sudden. The loss I feel and the sleepless nights and irritable days I have spent left me wondering if my behavior is normal—especially for an adult."

Pet lovers often resent the cool reception that their animals receive from nonowners; they resent it even more when their feelings over pet loss are taken lightly. The following comment in a letter from a pet owner is typical: "I'm happy to see pet loss treated with the importance that it deserves, rather than the trivialization which I observe in my non-pet-centered friends and acquaintances."

Mental health professionals find that their patients are often embarrassed when they discuss their feelings about pet loss, even though they are willing to talk about many more intimate matters. One clinical psychologist in New York reported that she had two patients who were trying to cope with the unexpected news of rapidly advancing cancer in much-beloved pets. They were ashamed to admit to friends, co-workers, and initially even to her how much they felt, "fearing to be mocked or considered weird." She had to stress repeatedly that their reactions were completely appropriate.

Psychologists and pet owners know that the human-pet connection is so strong that a pet's death can have a marked effect on one's physical and emotional well-being. The observation leads some specialists to believe that people often respond to human loss and pet loss in parallel ways, moving through similar stages of grief reactions.

Dealing with Loss

Dealing with loss is never easy, but it can be managed better through the following ways:

First—Knowing what to expect in the way of typical grief reactions and the stages of mourning.

Second—Learning ways of coping with grief reactions and accepting the length of time it takes to grieve.

Third—Recognizing the things that hold people back from recovery, such as abnormal grieving reactions and fear of grieving.

Fourth—Recognizing the signs of recovery.

These guidelines are explored in the following pages:

Typical Grief Reactions

The characteristic reactions that accompany a meaningful loss are familiar to most of us. We cry until we think there are no more tears left and then we cry again. We tend to feel disorganized. On the one hand, we are depressed and apathetic; the things that normally interest us don't seem to matter. On the other hand, we feel angry and guilty. When dealing with the death of a pet, we resent the animal for abandoning us, we resent people who don't understand our painful reactions, and we even resent others who have healthy pets. We make them feel "wrong" for our pet dying. We also feel guilty, reasonably or unreasonably, for not having done enough to save the loved animal.

Grief also invades our lives with persistent fears, nightmares, flashbacks of the deceased and problems of concentrating at work or in school. We can also react to grief in physical ways, with fatigue, loss of appetite, headaches, sleeplessness, nervousness, difficulty in breathing and other anxiety symptoms.

Of course, grief reactions vary in type and intensity from one person to another. Often the way we react depends upon the circumstances surrounding the pet's death, the depth of our attachment, our past history in dealing with loss, and our state of mind at the time of the event.

Stages of Grief

While there are great individual variations in grief responses, in general, grieving follows a pattern of stages from initial numbness to eventual recovery.

First Stage: Numbness

Immediately after a loss, most people react with shocked disbelief. Whether the pet's death was sudden or expected, it doesn't seem real. The numb feelings are a way we have of protecting ourselves from the full impact of the loss. The period of numbness is temporary, usually lasting a few hours or a day or so. Veterinarians say they often see owners who are dazed immediately after they learn of their pet's death.

"It simply doesn't register," observed Dr. William Kay, Chief of Staff of the Animal Medical Center in New York City. "Some people aren't equipped to handle the reality of death all at once. They wrap themselves in a curtain of disbelief to protect themselves, and pull it open only after they feel they can accept the truth."

One veterinarian recalled the story of James, a bachelor in his mid-forties who lived alone with his mixed retriever, Sheila. The dog was referred to the animal hospital with pyometria, a serious disease that required surgery. By James's own admission, his whole life centered around his pet, and he expressed his fear for her life in many phone calls to the veterinarian. As it turned out, the operation was successful and James was able to take Sheila home. Shortly afterward, however, the animal developed severe parvo virus infection, which necessitated her return to the hospital. Once again James flooded the hospital staff with phone calls about his pet's condition. He was assured that she was doing well following her treatment for shock and that he could take her home in just a few days. But on the morning that she was to be discharged, Sheila took several steps out of her cage, collapsed, and died instantly.

When the hospital called James with the sad news, he refused to believe it. He phoned repeatedly that morning, insisting that a mistake had been made. He simply could not accept the fact that his pet had died. James's actions seem irrational unless we understand that he was temporarily denying the event to give himself time to regain his balance.

Second Stage: Painful Feelings

Anger   When the shock and numbness wear off, we are often overwhelmed by anger. In James's case, he was so outraged that he threatened to kill one of the interns who had cared for his dog. A few days later he urged that the director of the hospital fire all the doctors involved. The following week he called to go over the entire episode again.

Although few people will have the extreme reactions displayed by James, it is common to feel anger when something we love is taken away from us. We feel angry at the pet for abandoning us and we also look for someone to blame. We turn our anger onto the veterinarian, or the driver of the car that ran over our animal, or the person who let the dog or cat out. Eventually, if the circumstances were unavoidable, we begin to recognize that our anger is not really justified—in fact, it might even have been irrational. Once we recognize that the true basis for the anger was our pet's abandoning us, we can deal with it, and the anger begins to fade.

Guilt   In addition to episodes of anger after the numbness wears off, there may be considerable guilt. It is not uncommon for people to feel they were responsible for the pet's loss or could have done more to save the animal's life. At times, the guilt may be justified, as in cases of neglect or willful malice toward a pet, but much of the time it is not.

For example, there is no one to blame for an injury that occurs if a cat darts out when a guest leaves a door open, or a dog slips its leash on an airing. These and many other circumstances are basic risks of pet ownership and have nothing to do with improper care. Animals do not reason or think abstractly the way human beings do, and they often act on impulse. Pets are subject to many perils in their daily lives, and we cannot control all of their actions.

Depression   Many times depression accompanies guilt because of the low self-esteem and the need for self-blame and self-punishment that people have in response to their inability to save their pet. The depression can last for days, weeks or months, and may interfere with everyday functioning. It usually brings about feelings of helplessness, powerlessness, loss of appetite, sleep troubles and a general lack of interest in daily matters. In most people guilt and depression will lift with time. A person who remains severely depressed or guilt-ridden continuously and for a long period of time should seek professional help to understand why these symptoms persist.

Grief Pangs   There is a tendency to feel what Colin Murray Parkes calls "pangs of grief." Our pet is sorely missed and we undergo periods of intense anxiety often marked by uncontrolled crying. Parkes observed that pangs of grief, or pining, generally begin "within a few hours or days of bereavement and usually reach a peak of severity within fourteen days. At first they are frequent and seem to occur spontaneously but as time passes they become less frequent and take place only when something occurs to bring the loss to mind."

These episodes of grief are also marked by restlessness, preoccupation with the deceased, and lack of concentration on the usual things that give us pleasure. It is as though we are searching for a lost object. Distressing as these reactions are, one can be reassured that they are natural and expected responses.

Coping with Your Grief

Ways to Cope

During the mourning period, there are two tasks that must be accomplished: the first is to acknowledge that the death has taken place and the relationship is over; the second is to deal with the feelings and changes that the loss creates.

Going over various events associated with your pet is effective in helping you to accept the reality of the loss. For example, you can reminisce about the good times and the bad, relate to other pets ("That dog looks just like Missy"), look at pictures of the animal and talk about all the ways the dog or cat contributed to your life. Returning to sites like a playground, a path in the woods or other places shared by the deceased pet is a common occasion of grief, and an opportunity to further the process of mourning.

Dealing with your feelings is another matter, because you can't perform acts that will chase them away. The emptiness that comes from sudden changes in daily routines, the loneliness from missing a loved companion, the feeling of uneasiness without the protector are to be expected. You may want to fight off these feelings, but it is better to experience them until they become less apparent in your life.

Another way to manage your feelings is to reach out to others for support. Caring friends can be good listeners, they can help comfort you and they can help you in daily routines that you might feel too upset to perform. It is particularly important for people who rely on their pets as their most significant source of companionship to be able to turn to friends and family immediately after the loss. The presence of visitors helps to fill the deep void left by the pet's death. Visits, or even telephone calls, from friends also help to confirm the significance of the loss—that a loved cat or a dog is worth grieving over.

How Long Does Grieving Last?

One of the most frequently asked and difficult questions to answer is how long grief should last. This is similar to asking how high is up. There are no limitations: for some people grieving over a pet lasts just a few days, but for others it can take weeks or even months, as the following letter describes:

> My husband and I lost our pet cat to euthanasia two and a half months ago after a prolonged illness due to kidney failure. My husband is handling it well with only occasional loss feelings. I don't feel I am handling it as well. I even feel some resentment at the ease of my husband's transition. We have no intention of finding a replacement for our lost pet. Clinically we know that there was nothing more that could humanly be done and he was buried in a dignified manner. Yet, I feel periods of extreme guilt, grief, physical loss and from time to time suffer nightmares.
>
> I have my most difficult periods when the events of his death replay in my mind and in handling the knowledge of his physical decomposition. I would be most appreciative for the reassurance that this hurt will lessen in time, as it seems only marginally improved after two and a half months.
>
> —Sara R.

Sara is concerned that her grief reactions have gone on too long, but in fact hers is an appropriate response. People's emotional repair systems differ; some need more time and support than others.

The grief reaction and the length of time it takes to recover depend on several factors: the age of the pet; the length of time it was owned; the degree of attachment to the pet; whether the death was sudden or anticipated; and whether the pet was euthanized. But the most important factor is how well the person can deal with separation openly and realistically. While grief has no time limit, the reactions should begin to become less noticeable as time goes on. That is the signal to let us know that we are on the way to recovery.

Barriers to Recovery

Abnormal Grief

Some individuals suffer from exaggerated or prolonged grief, in which bereavement continues unrelieved for indefinite periods of time. These reactions arise from an inability to give up the lost pet because the need for the animal's companionship is so intense. The following letter describes such a situation:

> I am a middle-aged teacher who never has recovered from the death of Apricot, a seventeen-year-old poodle who had to be put to sleep. This happened four years ago and I was sedated for days. Two weeks later I acquired a baby cocker spaniel. He was never off a leash but slipped his collar one night while I was walking him. He ran into the road, me after him, but he was killed instantly by a drunken driver. I was out of school for two weeks. However, the day after the accident my husband insisted we buy another cocker—a little girl. She is now two and I am a nervous wreck, lest something happen to her. She is beautiful, spoiled, but very quiet and well-behaved. My vacations have to be in motels that allow little pups. She is first in everything. My husband is fond of her, but not like myself. I still get upset on the other two dogs' birthdays and anniversaries of their deaths. Dog lovers understand; others think I am a nut.
>
> —Maris S.

Another example of exaggerated grief is presented in the following letter:

> My sister Gloria is having very real difficulties in dealing with the deaths of our animals, to a point of severe depression. She recently has been very ill and this may have been part of a culmination of some severe problems with regard to our dog

Freckles who died from epilepsy. My sister became very depressed and the situation has gotten worse as time goes on. At this time she virtually panics when someone even shows signs of being ill. We would appreciate having help with this pervasive problem.

—T.W.

In both of these cases, the normal mourning process has been interfered with and professional help could be beneficial. Some people simply cannot recover from grief on their own; something is holding them back from facing their feelings. They need the support and guidance of trained personnel to help them work through their grief in order to function effectively.

Through therapy, the bereaved are encouraged to recall and recount in great detail all of the events leading up to the loss, the circumstances surrounding it and their subsequent experiences. In this way a bereaved person can sort out hopes, despairs, regrets, anxiety, anger and guilt, and begin to view the loss in terms of what it actually means to their lives.

Fear of Grieving

Although grieving is the recognized way of dealing effectively with loss, there are many people who are afraid to grieve. They are confused by the flood of feelings that follow a loss. They feel out of control and helpless and do not see an end to their painful reactions. They sometimes think they are "going mad" although in fact their reactions are generally quite normal.

The tendency not to deal with grief can mean that painful reactions crop up at some time in the future—when they are least expected or desired. Often they arise when we suffer another loss. We then have the burden of mourning the passing of two loved ones.

Signs of Recovery

Recovery begins when thoughts of the loved animal move from the foreground to the background of our minds. As the focus shifts we can think of the pet with love but without pain. We can reminisce, we can look at photographs, we can talk about the pet and it hurts less and less. Of course, there are times when we actively miss our dog or cat—the daily jog, cuddling up on a cold night—and the periods of grieving recur. It takes time to release ourselves from these attachments.

A further sign of recovery is the ability to establish new relationships. In many cases this means replacing the pet; on the other hand, it can mean deciding that a new pet is inappropriate. The healthy sign here is the absence of confused feelings. (The situation is discussed in Chapter 7.)

To deal with your grief, it is necessary to understand why you miss your pet so much, and what exactly your attachments were based on. Then you must allow yourself to express all of your feelings about your animal and what the loss meant to you; and you must also accept the reality of your pet's death. Once this is accomplished, and you begin to view the loss without pain, you can begin to establish new relationships. When the time comes that your sorrow disappears but your love and fond memories remain, you will have completed the grieving process.

It is important to recognize that different people are affected by loss in different ways, that there is no clearcut time limit to grieving, and that the intensity of grief very often corresponds with the degree of attachment and the circumstances surrounding the pets's death. In time, the fact that a pet lived becomes more important than the fact that a pet died. Above all, it helps to remember that grieving over a lost pet is an entirely natural and appropriate reaction that is governed by one's inner feelings.

3   Helping Children with Pet Loss

It is hard to imagine a more natural and openhearted attachment than the one between children and their pets. As adults, we often concern ourselves with the responsibility of pet ownership, but children rarely allow their love to be affected by worry or cost. They simply and naïvely give their affection to the family pet—who is probably the most unconditionally accepting figure in their lives.

When a loved pet dies, a whole world may open up to a child: a world of loss, grief, bereavement and confusion about how to handle this first experience with death. It is often a troublesome time for parents as well, who may be dealing with their own feelings, while trying to help their children. A young mother wrote: "When our family cat died a few weeks ago, we were all terribly distressed. But my main concern is my four-year-old twins. They were immediately worried that if the cat, who was always around, could die, so could we, their parents. Then they would be alone. Now their major problem is finality. They keep wondering why the cat can't come back."

How these and other difficult questions are treated, and what children observe in the actions of the adults around them, will have an important influence on the way they handle loss in the future. It makes a great deal of difference whether children see reaction to loss treated openly, realistically and supportively, or as something to be hidden or avoided. These first experiences make up the "memory bank" for handling future losses. They will be called upon over and over again throughout life.

Helping Children Deal with Pet Loss

In order to help their children cope with loss effectively, parents need to be aware of several factors: what role the pet played in the child's life; the ways children react to loss; and how children view death at different ages. Following a discussion of these matters, there are practical suggestions about breaking the news of the pet's death or impending death; guidelines on handling questions and explanations; suggested activities to help children with their grief; the role of the teacher; handling funeral and burial arrangements; and replacing a pet.

What Pets Mean To Children

The nondemanding, nonjudgmental nature of the family pet makes it a valuable friend for a youngster. Children cannot possibly measure up at all times to the standards set by others; they are bound occasionally to disappoint their parents, teachers, siblings and friends. But not the family pet. The loyal cat or dog is not bothered by dirty hands at the dinner table, a poor report card or cheating at games. Not even a galloping case of chicken pox can keep a dog or cat from cuddling up and reassuring a child that he is worth loving.

Pets fulfill other important needs for children in addition to love and companionship. Caring for the cat or dog is the one task that most children can perform on a par with their parents or older siblings. Small children feel important when they are given the responsibility of feeding the cat or walking the dog. And the sense of self-esteem often spills over into other areas of their lives. Being a pet owner also gives a child a feeling of belonging and a sense of pride. Furthermore, children derive a sense of security from the protection that many pets provide.

Some specialists have observed that pets may promote emotional stability in very young children. Normally infants show signs of distress when they are separated from their mothers and handed over to other caregivers. According to the psychologist Boris Levinson, having a pet as a constant companion may help ease the baby's distress "by providing for that otherwise unavailable continuity which is so important in the development of trust in the world and oneself."

Having a cat or a dog may also promote a child's physical development. Many a baby has gained the incentive to crawl or to walk following a pet around; and older children can release a great deal of physical energy by exercising or roughhousing with their animals.

Pets frequently serve as objects of fantasy, allowing children to strengthen their imaginations by making up stories about themselves and their animal companions. Moreover, a dog or cat may also serve as a scapegoat ("It was Duffy who wrinkled up my homework") and provide excuses ("I can't do the dishes—I have to take Chucky out for a walk").

Children up to the age of about five or so miss the deceased dog or cat, but more as a playmate than as an object that satisfies their basic emotional needs. These are still being fulfilled by parents and other caregivers. It is older children and adolescents who generally bear the brunt of pet loss. The uncritical, accepting nature of the dog or cat is extremely important to these young people, who are beginning to experience alienation and rebellion in their relationships with the authority figures in their lives.

Moreover, many adolescents have difficulty in showing physical affection to others, as they try to establish themselves as independent individuals. Many believe that it is "unmanly" or "babyish" to bestow signs of caring on family members. In such cases pets serve as wonderful outlets. Most adolescents feel perfectly comfortable rolling on the floor or cuddling with the family cat or dog. With the pet's death, a highly acceptable means of showing and receiving affection is gone.

Symptoms of Grief in Children

Children respond to death and loss in many of the same ways as adults: with disbelief and denial at first and then with crying, bewilderment, anger, guilt, depression and attempts to rationalize the loss (see Chapter 2). Some symptoms are more common with children: fear of abandonment, nightmares, insomnia and anger toward siblings and playmates. Children can also develop learning problems in school stemming from lack of concentration brought on by anxiety. There is often a great deal of guilt because a child has indulged in "magical thinking." The youngster may have wished at some point for the pet to leave or die: when this happens the child attributes the loss to these thoughts. Some children may feel that they are being punished because of their wishes.

Very often children do not indicate the depth of their grief verbally, so parents must be on the lookout for unusual behavior. This can occur weeks after the loss, as seen in the following case history:

When the dog belonging to nine-year-old Janie died suddenly, she showed common reactions of crying and sleeplessness for the first few days. Then the symptoms disappeared. While her parents were sympathetic, they were not very attached to the animal; they treated the loss matter-of-factly and were not surprised when Janie seemed to recover quickly.

A week or so later, however, they noticed that their daughter seemed listless, preoccupied and unable to concentrate at school or home. Something was terribly wrong with their normally cheerful fourth-grader, but they couldn't discover the cause.

When the behavior continued for more than a month, Janie's mother talked over the problem with a psychiatrist. The doctor asked about any unusual events in the little girl's life and finally learned about the animal's death. "But it was just a mongrel," explained her mother. "I don't think Janie was very attached to the dog. She only had it for a year. She found it on the street." After just a session or two with Janie, the therapist learned the cause for the depression: if Harpo could die suddenly and nobody much cared, then, Janie reasoned, she could die suddenly too, without being mourned. With a great deal of reassurance that in the highly unlikely event of her death, she would be sorely missed, Janie's depression eventually disappeared. Her parents had simply not realized the extent of their daughter's grief and hidden anxiety.

Of course, grief symptoms vary with the individual child, depending upon the strength of the attachment, how long the pet had been in the family, the circumstances surrounding the animal's death (see Chapters 4 and 5) and the child's emotional makeup.

The time it takes to recover from grief reactions depends upon many of these same factors, in addition to how well parents and children accept the symptoms, regard them as natural and deal with them openly. It is important to remember that while there is no time limit to grieving, eventually the symptoms should start fading. If they continue unrelieved, you should consider professional help for your child.

Children's Views of Loss and Death

Children deal with separation and death in different ways, depending upon their ages, emotional growth and individual personalities. It is helpful for parents to understand these differences so they may key their discussions about the pet's death to the child's level of comprehension.

Children up to the age of five or so generally do not view death or loss as permanent. Rather, they look upon it as a temporary absence, similar to the phenomenon of the plant that "dies" one year only to return the next in full bloom. Some preschool youngsters view death as a deep sleep or other condition of absence.

From the ages of about five to nine, children tend to personify death in some way—perhaps as a "separate person" (like the grim reaper). Although children at this stage know there is a definite difference between life and death, there is also the fantasy that death can be avoided and that it is not a necessary experience for everyone.

The last phase begins when children reach the age of nine or ten. They begin to have an adult perception that death is final, permanent and inevitable. This can cause increased anxiety in some children, and a preoccupation with being abandoned whether through death or other separation such as divorce.

Informing Children of a Pet's Death

In light of the young child's low level of understanding, up to the age of five it is more important to provide support than explanations. However, some preschoolers might be prepared to deal with elementary explanations such as: "Sometimes when a pet gets very sick it cannot stay where it lives anymore. That's what happened to Blackie. But we're here and we're not leaving." From the age of about six on the child should be told as directly as possible that the pet has died and about the circumstances surrounding the death. However, it is not advisable to go into morbid details—such information is what nightmares are made of. It is important to encourage questions at this time and to provide sympathetic, straightforward answers.

One of the most frequently asked questions from parents is what to do when children are away at camp or school or on vacation, and the pet either dies suddenly or becomes so ill that euthanasia is warranted. As preparation, the child should be told initially that the animal has been very sick or injured. If the child asks directly whether the pet has died or will do so soon, answer honestly. Otherwise, if you can wait a week or so before breaking the news of the pet's death, your child will have time to get accustomed to the possibility.

If a pet is to be euthanized, wait, if possible, until your child returns home so the family can be together. Under no circumstances should you lie to your child. Here is a letter from a mother describing how her family handled the situation:

> This past summer, three weeks before our children, aged fourteen, twelve and ten, returned home from camp, we discovered that Lucky, our eleven-year-old poodle, had inoperable bone cancer in her rear leg and could not survive. On visiting day we told Tim and Nancy, the two older children, what the situation was and what the outcome would be. The youngest, Bert, was told only that Lucky was very, very sick.
>
> We wanted to wait until Bert came home to tell him about the finality of the situation. We knew how attached he was to Lucky and how crushed he would be. We wanted to be able to comfort him and cry with him rather than have him learn the news while in camp.
>
> Lucky was euthanized a few days after the children arrived home. It was a very sad event for all of us, but the children agreed that they needed to say good-bye to her and would have been terribly angry if we had euthanized her while they were at camp to spare them. Most of our friends advised us to do it while the children were away; I'm glad we didn't take that advice.

Of course, every family situation is different and sometimes it is impossible to delay the course of action. No matter how the situation is handled, your support and understanding, whether you feel touched by the loss or not, are essential.

Do's and Don'ts in Handling Discussions and Questions

Among the first questions a child will ask are: "Why did the pet die?" "Did I do something wrong?" "What will happen to the pet now?" The answers, of course, will vary according to circumstances, but the key is to reply as directly and supportively as possible. Here are some do's and don'ts that might help parents in handling these and other difficult questions.

DO offer explanations that are clear and understandable and ones that you feel comfortable with, in language familiar to the child. The point of your explanation should be that unfortunate things occur despite all of our love and care. There are some things we have no control over. We know nothing lasts forever.

DON'T offer explanations that have the potential for causing additional psychological problems, such as:

"The pet ran away and won't be coming back." This tends to make rejection and abandonment fantasies worse in the child.

"The pet went to sleep." This might well result in sleep problems, with the child fearful of meeting the same fate as the cat or dog.

"The pet didn't like it here so it went away." This also provokes feelings of guilt and rejection.

"The pet was sick and died," without adding immediately that being sick doesn't have to lead to dying. Otherwise the child might become extraordinarily fearful of illness.

"The pet was very sick and the vet had to make it die." Here you
are making a negative association between a caregiver and
the taking away of life.

DO let your child know that grief and mourning are normal. Such reassurance is essential in helping a youngster to
cope with the painful feelings.

DO allow your child to openly show and share feelings, no
matter how irrational or silly they may seem. Children
should be encouraged to bring their anger, disappointment
and tears out into the open.

DON'T stifle your child's feelings by remarks such as "Big
boys and girls don't cry," or "It's only an animal, we'll get
another one."

DO be aware of your own feelings and reactions in response to the death of the pet. Even if you are not very
moved by the loss, put yourself in your child's place.

DO provide as positive and appropriate a model as you
can, keeping in mind that a child will look to an adult for
direction and guidance.

DO communicate to your child that you understand.

Suggested Activities

There are certain activities that will help encourage your
child's expression of grief, a task that must be accomplished
in order to move toward recovery. Look through photograph
albums for pictures of the dog or cat and have one framed if
your child would like it, to keep the pet's memory alive. Talk
about the days when the pet first came into the family, reminisce about shows or ribbons, how hard it was to train the pet
and the funny habits it developed.

One of the best activities to encourage the expression of
grief is for children to put their thoughts down on paper.

Following is an example of how ten-year-old Bert, the youngster whose dog Lucky was to be euthanized, put his feelings into words:

Why? Why? It's all Dr. Smith's fault. He could have found it sooner. Then we could amputate her leg and she would be with us for two more years. Why did it have to be her? It's like a nightmare. It's too sad for me. She'll never know what I'll look like with my teeth all fixed and my braces off. Only three days. She looks so healthy. Cancer. You told me just straight out. Couldn't you be more gentle? I feel angry and mad and sad altogether. Why Lucky? I'm going to feel so sad when I come home from school and she isn't there to greet me. I always liked to lie down with her when I finished playing. I don't want her to go away from me. I like to fluff her ears. Remember how she used to chase a diaper. My stomach hurts. I'll never love another dog as much.

In the above, Bert goes through a number of common grief reactions: the initial feelings of anger—blaming the veterinarian for Lucky's illness; the fantasy about what could be done to save the dog (amputation); the questions about why it had to be Lucky; and the reminiscences of his pet. By putting his thoughts and feelings into words, Bert is releasing his sorrow. Once it is out in the open, grief is much easier to manage.

Books that deal with the subject of pet loss can contribute to your child's understanding of the experience. Good examples for younger children are *The Dead Bird*, a picture book by Margaret Brown, and *The Tenth Best Thing about Barney*, a book by Judith Viorst that deals with the death of a loved cat. Suggested reading for older children include *The Accident*, by Carol Carrick, a story about a pet dog's sudden death; *Bristle Face*, by Zachary Balls, a book that deals with the mercy killing of a blinded pet dog; and *The Yearling*, by Marjorie Rawlings, which sensitively treats the subject of a pet fawn that must be killed for the sake of the family's survival. Librarians can be helpful in directing you and your children to other appropriate reading material.

The Role of the Teacher

Notifying your child's teacher will serve several purposes. When professional educators are alerted to problems stemming from events at home, they are prepared to handle children with special care; without this information, your child's wandering attention, short temper or other behavior problems arising from the loss might be misunderstood. The teacher can also be on the lookout for, and alert you to, unusual behavior that crops up weeks after the loss. Moreover, a teacher can integrate the event into classroom activities. For example, a discussion about pets and pet loss allows a child to recognize that the problem is worth discussing and chances are that it has been shared by others in the class.

This letter from a teacher is illustrative:

> Marty came to class today very upset and crying. When I approached him he said his dog died last night. My heart certainly went out to this young man, as I, too, am a great animal lover. We discussed Marty's feelings and talked about the possibility of a new dog. I assured him that animals certainly do count and they certainly mean a great deal to their masters.

This teacher's sensitivity and support will go a long way toward helping Marty manage his emotions.

Burial and Funeral Arrangements

Children should be asked if they have any special requests for burial or funeral services, and their wishes should be followed if at all possible. Knowing where the pet is buried helps to remove a great deal of the mystery surrounding death. (Chapter 6 deals with the options for burial or cremation.)

Replacement

It is a good idea to delay making plans about pet replacement until the opportunity has arisen to speak about it in depth. Some children are not ready to substitute a new animal for a loved pet, while others find it important to do so quickly. The subject of replacement is discussed in Chapter 7.

The major tasks we as parents need to accomplish in helping our children manage pet loss is to assure them that their grief reactions are normal, to allow the expressions of that grief, to encourage questions, to provide straightforward and sympathetic answers and explanations, and to set a positive model for our children to follow. By supporting and comforting them as they grapple and mourn, we are guiding them through a difficult period. And we are helping them to lay the groundwork for dealing with subsequent losses throughout their lives.

4 When a Pet Dies Suddenly

As in many longstanding relationships, we tend to assume that our pets will be with us indefinitely. The sudden death of a loved animal, catching us unaware and unprepared, is very likely to cause especially profound grief reactions.

A death that is preceded by neither a long illness nor advancing age means that one has had no time to adjust to impending loss. The immediate necessity to quickly make the plans and decisions required by the pet's death, while at the same time dealing with the unexpected grief, is especially stressful.

In many cases, the sudden death is due to an accident or physical attack—and this can intensify an owner's emotional reaction. Not only does the violence make one shudder, and perhaps bring feelings of helplessness or of violation, but the thought of negligence can cause one to replay again and again the circumstances surrounding the death, imagining different endings.

This tendency to think "If only . . ." is a painful but natural response; eventually most people gain perspective and stop sorting through all the possible actions they might have taken and realize that what happened, happened. The circumstances may have been beyond their control.

Sudden death, even from natural causes, can be the occasion for intense distress. The following letter expresses some of the feelings of disruption and emptiness caused by the unexpected loss:

I lost my beloved Cocoa—an eight-year-old mixed-breed retriever and shepherd—unexpectedly several months ago. She hadn't slowed down or stopped eating nor did she show any signs of unusual behavior. In fact, the day she died she was acting quite normally. But that afternoon, when she stretched out on the floor to take a nap, she gave a loud sigh and died. It was so sudden.

Cocoa really gave my life a purpose. My four children are grown and gone now. I am fifty-seven years old and I thought my beloved Cocoa and I could grow old together. Now when I get ready for work there is no one to watch me, or wait for me when I return. I feel so empty coming home. How does one accept the tragedy of losing a wonderful pet?

—Jennifer P.

This owner had been prepared to accept the absence of her children; it was the natural order for them to grow up and leave. But Cocoa was a different matter. She had counted on her pet's companionship; suddenly the dog was gone without even giving her a chance to say a proper good-bye. The unfinished business added to her sense of loss.

The ways in which people tend to react over sudden pet loss, practical suggestions for dealing with emergencies, and the legal recourses one has when a pet's death is due to negligence are examined in the following pages.

Stages of Grief Reaction

Sudden and premature loss leads to great shock and not infrequently denial, which is the mind's way of helping to cope with the loss. "I don't believe it" is the first thing we say. Or "It's not true, it couldn't have happened."

Habits are hard to break at this time: we unthinkingly reach for the leash after breakfast for the morning walk or automatically open the cabinet, looking for the cat food. We are aware of the loss, but a part of us refuses to let go. It is our way of protecting ourselves, at first, from the full impact of the loss.

This period of shock and denial, which generally lasts a few days, is often followed by separation anxiety. The loneliness becomes exaggerated as one feels the pet's absence very strongly and focuses intensely on the loss to the exclusion of other matters—which frequently irritates family members or friends. During this period of anxiety one may also feel a sense of abandonment: "How could my pet have left me without warning? What did I do to deserve this?"

As the anxiety lessens, it is replaced by feelings of anger and guilt. In some cases, the anger can be justified: the veterinarian may, in fact, have misdiagnosed a sudden illness or a family member may have been careless with the cat or dog. But often the anger is misdirected toward the practitioner who failed to save the sick or injured animal that was beyond help, or at the driver who couldn't swerve to avoid the pet running under the wheels, or the person who unintentionally dropped the leash. In fact, the anger here is really felt toward the pet for leaving so suddenly.

Feelings of guilt may provoke self-blame or self-reproach—especially when the pet has died as the result of an accident. If the pet slipped out while the door was being answered, a reasonable owner can hardly blame himself. One can't be expected to lock up a pet inside the house because it shows signs of curiosity. But other situations may lead people to feel they abdicated their responsibility. Many times owners are busy or feeling unwell or lazy, and they let their pet go outside alone. Or they fail to open the door when the animal scratches to come in. After all, it had stayed out many times before with no harm done, and there was no reason to expect that the circumstances would be different. But if one's indifference to a pet's needs results in an accident, the burden of guilt may be heavy indeed.

One woman bluntly told her therapist: "I opened the door

and killed my pet." Not so, explained the therapist: "You may have opened the door, you may have let your poodle out, but you did that many times in the past. It was a calculated risk, and we all take them. You had no way of knowing that your dog would impulsively chase a garbage truck and be hit by an automobile. You cannot absolve yourself of blame, completely, of course, but you must put the act in perspective. Remember, you did not intentionally let your pet out to be killed. It was an accident and none of us is immune to them."

With time, as past memories are constantly challenged by reality and present needs, most people work through their guilt and anger and return to their normal lives.

Practical Advice for Dealing with Emergencies

The occurrences that can lead to a sudden death, such as vehicular accidents, acute illness, attack by other animals, shooting or poisoning, can temporarily immobilize a stunned owner. Many people are "frozen" by fear and unable to think clearly when confronted with the sight of a severely or fatally injured pet. The following pages provide practical advice if you face such a distressing and confusing episode. By being prepared in an emergency, you help yourself as well as your pet. No matter what the outcome of the accident, it is comforting to know that you did everything possible to save the loved pet.

Call the Veterinarian

Whether the animal is stricken at home or in the street, the first step is to make sure it is breathing. Emergency first aid given immediately after the accident could save the animal. (Owners should become familiar with principles of first aid as soon as they acquire a pet. Some good books on the subject are *First Aid for Pets,* by Robert W. Kirk, D.V.M.; *Your Pet's Health from A–Z,* by Donal B. McKeown, D.V.M.; and *Pet Medicine: Health Care and First Aid for All Household Pets,* by Roger A. Caras, et al., eds.

The next step is to call a veterinarian. It is preferable to contact the practitioner who has cared for the animal, but if he is unavailable, contact the covering veterinary physician or the closest animal emergency clinic. A veterinarian can assess the situation on the telephone and help you decide whether to take the injured animal to his office, to a medical center or a specialist. It is not a routine function of a veterinarian to make "house calls"; although this service is becoming more available now, you should not expect that a veterinarian will come to the scene. By describing as clearly as possible the circumstances and extent of injury, you will help the clinician to decide the best course of action.

There may be times, particularly at night, when your veterinarian cannot be reached. The regional animal hospital or local police department will be able to put you in touch with a qualified veterinarian. Since police officers normally are not trained to assess injuries or determine treatment for a sick animal, it is important to reach a veterinarian.

Transportation

It is likely that you will have to transport your sick or injured pet to the veterinarian's office or animal hospital. This can create a problem if you are alone: the animal may be heavy and you may be fearful of adding to the injury, frightening the pet, angering or increasing its pain in the process of moving it. If you pick it up and hurt its broken pelvis or leg it may bite. This can be dangerous because the animal in your arms is near your face and throat. If you need help, call an animal hospital, the police or an animal shelter organization; trained personnel will be able to suggest ways to move the injured animal and in some cases may offer physical help, although facilities, of course, differ in every community.

When Death Occurs

Even if your pet does not survive the injury or illness, it helps to act calmly and logically. If you have not decided in advance about burial procedures, alert the veterinarian's office that you will be bringing the animal there. Many veterinarians are prepared to keep your cat or dog until decisions about disposal are made. Or a shelter organization can usually provide the same service. The most practical way to transport the pet is in a blanket, sheet or pillow case. This is a time when you may need a great deal of help and support—do not hesitate to call on personnel at the veterinarian's office or animal shelter.

Legal Recourses

When the burial has been arranged and the initial shock is subsiding, some owners become so angry about the circumstances surrounding the death that they want to take legal action.

What can an owner do when his pet, leashed on his property, has been attacked by a dog known to be vicious? What if the animal died because of a veterinarian's negligence? Or was poisoned by contaminated pet food? Are there grounds for a successful lawsuit?

Legal doctrines vary from state to state, but with a few exceptions, the courts generally view pets as personal property—which means that in most cases, the only monetary reward that an owner can collect, no matter what the circumstances of death, is the fair market value of the animal. When suing for recovery, the owner must prove what the dog or cat would have brought on the market, based on its original price and the current value of animals of similar age, breed and sex. In the case of a pet used for breeding, or a show dog or cat, the owner would demonstrate the actual or potential income to be derived from the animal.

The emphasis on the commercial aspect of a pet's relationship with an owner strikes many people as coldhearted and unrealistic. Most pet lovers view their animals in terms of affection and companionship; it is rare to hear an owner, other than a breeder, discussing a pet's monetary value. According to attorneys for The Humane Society of the United States, there are some signs that the courts are beginning to share this view. In some cases, the courts have allowed an owner to recover for emotional distress, especially when an animal was killed deliberately. In other legal commentary, the pet has been seen as property that is analogous to a family heirloom, that is, worth more than its fair market value because of sentimental value.

The issue still remains of whether the outcome of a lawsuit will be large enough to make this legal step economically feasible. Another consideration is the time, effort and emotional energy involved in bringing suit, balanced against the need for getting even.

But monetary recovery aside, many people feel that it is their responsibility to lodge a complaint against the owner of a dog that has attacked their pet, because unless the animal is restricted by court order from wandering free, it may continue to harass other animals and possibly even humans. People who want to lodge a complaint do not necessarily have to go to court. Some localities have informal-disputes services in which the local prosecutor hears both sides and acts as mediator. This may avoid a full-blown legal suit.

The laws concerning dangerous animals vary widely. In general, the statutes are designed to protect human beings: with local twists and variations, most codes state that if a dog attacks an individual, the victim or a witness can destroy the dog at the time of the attack with no liability. Or the owner may be brought to court. When it comes to attacks on pets, the laws are much less specific.

In New York State, for example, the Agriculture and Markets Law of 1979 calls for the destruction of an offending dog if it "chases, attacks or worries any domestic animal which is any place where it may lawfully be." However, the law defines domestic animals as "sheep, horses, cattle, goats, swine, fowl, ducks, geese, swans, turkeys, confined hares, confined pheasants and other birds." There is no mention of cats or dogs. The law was intended to protect farm animals and give indemnity to owners, since these animals are known not to initiate attacks.

In general, it is up to the individual magistrate to decide whether a dog is vicious. If found to be so, the animal may be ordered removed, confined or destroyed, depending upon its past history.

When contemplating any legal action because of possible negligence in a pet's death, an attorney should be consulted. A lawsuit may or may not result in a significant monetary recovery; a complaint against a vicious animal may or may not be sustained and lead to a safer neighborhood. But exploring the possibilities for legal action, even if none is ever taken, helps to relieve the feelings of frustration, anger and helplessness that arise over the accidental or unexpected death of a pet.

Coping with the death of a pet is always difficult, but when the loss is unexpected, one may feel an even greater blow. The lack of preparation can leave an owner vulnerable; he is not ready to let go. After reality takes hold one often feels angry. The hostility may be directed at the caretaker who allowed the accident to happen, at the veterinarian who couldn't save the pet and most of all at the pet itself for leaving so suddenly.

Guilt, which often accompanies a loss, is particularly pronounced in a sudden, accidental death. One imagines the event could have been avoided and so the guilt is fed by reviewing the event and fantasizing different endings. The key to relieving these symptoms is to recognize that the accident was not intentional and that some circumstances are beyond one's control. In cases of negligence, accepting the responsibility may help ease the feelings of guilt.

5   Euthanasia: A Dilemma

The decision to end an animal's life through euthanasia is probably the most difficult one we face as responsible pet owners. Conflicting questions produce uncertainty: Isn't it true that everything alive has a will to live? Yet, aren't there times when pain and suffering should be ended? Is it properly within our power to decide the fate of another living creature? Can we bring ourselves to voluntarily give up our pet?

These questions pose a dilemma because there are no right or wrong answers. The sensitive issue of euthanasia is a matter of personal judgment.

However, there are many factors that can influence the decision, including the pet's physical condition, the veterinarian's recommendation and our own moral views on the issue. These considerations will be examined in the following pages, along with an evaluation of the methods used in euthanasia; a discussion of whether owners should participate in the procedure; and advice about making satisfactory arrangements for euthanasia. We will also explore some of the feelings that frequently follow euthanasia.

Making the Decision

Among the many factors that enter the decision-making process, pet owners are probably influenced the most by the quality of life their pet can lead, despite being sick or infirm. The following stories illustrate two contrasting situations:

Ever since Cinnamon, a thirteen-year-old cocker spaniel, developed severe arthritis, she needed a great deal of assistance to move around. Three times a day, her owners carried her down the steps leading outside so that she could relieve herself. In the mild weather Cinnamon stayed outdoors, settling under an ancient oak tree; when it was cold she curled up near the kitchen stove. Her family affectionately called her the dowager queen.

There was no question that Cinnamon was in some pain, but according to the veterinarian it was neither continuous nor severe, and could be controlled with medication. With her family's help, Cinnamon quietly enjoyed her remaining time, and eventually ended her days naturally.

Sphinx, a Siamese who was suffering from leukemia, faced a quite different situation. The disease had left its mark: the once-beautiful cat was thin and worn, his eyes were failing and he could barely walk. It was obvious to Sphinx's owner, a young woman who had raised him from a kitten, that her cat was suffering terribly. Sally's veterinarian told her that the cat had little chance of recovering. While he could be kept alive on drugs, his pain would continue to worsen. Although the day Sally decided to put Sphinx away is one of the saddest she can recall, she also believed the decision was the kindest one she could have made for her cat.

These are obviously two extreme cases. If your situation is as clearcut, your course of action may be relatively uncomplicated. The "gray area" cases are the ones that fill owners with uncertainty. At times the cat or dog may be comfortable, bright and alert; at other times, lethargic and in pain. On "good days," you may consider euthanasia unthinkable. But on the difficult days it may seem like the best answer. You may be helped in your decision by judging your pet's ability to function. If your cat or dog can no longer do the things it once enjoyed, if it can't respond in the usual ways, if there is more pain than pleasure in its life—these are the evaluations that may influence your decision.

There are other factors that enter into the decision, as well. What is a family with growing children to do, for example, when an aging or sickly pet becomes bad-tempered and has a tendency to nip, scratch or turn on visitors? Or if the animal cannot control its bodily functions and frequently relieves itself in the house? These and other signs of advancing age and sickness present problems in the household. Sometimes a veterinarian can improve an animal's temperament or incontinence with drugs. But if these traits continue, the pet's presence may markedly decrease your own quality of life.

Sometimes cost is a factor in keeping a pet alive. Can you afford the expense of surgery on an aging pet? Among your considerations, of course, will be the pet's chance for survival and recovery. But the family budget must also be taken into account if the cost of medication and postoperative care will cause economic strain.

There are some people who turn to euthanasia because they do not want the burden of caring for a sickly pet. The animal may need walking more often than usual or frequent medication and attention. A pet with diabetes, for instance, often requires a daily urine test. Caring for the pet may necessitate returning home from work in the middle of the day or hiring a pet sitter.

In any consideration of euthanasia, the role of the veterinarian is crucial in outlining symptoms, determining medication, and informing the owners about the degree of pain and the course of the illness. While veterinarians must accept the responsibility for ensuring that only humane methods will be used, the final decision for euthanasia must be made by the owner.

If you have doubts about the veterinarian's recommendation, seek a second or third opinion, if necessary. If you live alone you might want to talk the matter over with a trusted friend or relative who shares your feelings about pets. When there are children in the household who you believe are old enough to understand make it a family discussion. The children contributed to the pet's care and may want to express their feelings or opinions. (Some youngsters accept euthanasia more easily than adults. They do not want to see their pet in pain and they are not weighed down by the responsibility of the final decision.) When explaining the situation to a child, be careful not to put the burden on the veterinarian. This creates a negative connection between death and the medical profession. (See Chapter 3 for help in explaining pet loss to children.)

After considering the veterinarian's evaluation and discussing the matter with family or friends, you should contact the animal doctor again if you still have questions. You should be absolutely certain in your own mind that you are doing the right thing for your pet.

In writing about this subject in *McCall's* magazine, Dr. Michael Fox, a noted animal behaviorist, gave his criteria for euthanizing an animal: "When *should* a pet be put away and for what reason? Should any aged or sick animal that is not suffering unduly be kept alive as long as possible on supportive medication? I say, if it is *certain* that the pet is not in pain and if you can afford the medication without great financial hardship, of course, support your pet's life as long as possible. However, if an animal has an incurable illness and is in great pain, I see no reason for keeping it alive. And if the cost of caring for a very sick or injured pet is so great that it is an acute strain on the family budget, then euthanasia may be the only answer."

A Guide to Methods of Euthanasia

If you decide that there is no alternative but to euthanize your animal, there are certain facts you should know about the methods that are commonly used. A veterinarian or animal shelter should accomplish euthanasia in the most humane way: by rendering the cat or dog unconscious and insensitive to pain as quickly as possible, without inducing anxiety or fear in the animal. The means of producing humane death may differ when animals are handled in a group rather than individually, but should meet these criteria. It should be noted, however, that the group method has been roundly criticized as unsatisfactory by many veterinarians.

Whether you are planning to bring your pet to a veterinarian or to an animal shelter, inquire about the technique to be used. If you are not satisfied, seriously consider changing the source. Even if it costs a little more, it will insure your peace of mind to know that you ended your pet's life in the most humane way possible.

The evaluation of methods for euthanasia that follows is based on information from a 1978 report by the American Veterinary Medical Association Panel on Euthanasia. (It should be kept in mind that findings may change in light of further investigation.)

Most Acceptable

It is generally agreed by specialists that an overdose of a barbiturate, such as sodium pentobarbital, is the preferred method. An overdose will render the animal unconscious within seconds, depress the central nervous system and lead to arrested breathing and cessation of heart action, resulting in death. An experienced veterinarian, who had tried other methods, said that sodium pentobarbital is the only method she will now use: "The animal literally 'goes to sleep.' The drug does not create a reaction in the pet that can be frightening to owners who are present. An overdose of barbiturate administered intravenously is quick, painless and very dignified."

Some veterinarians use a nonbarbiturate drug called T-61, a muscle relaxant and anesthetic. According to the American Veterinary Medical Association panel, a comparative study of T-61 and pentobarbital showed that either agent produces euthanasia smoothly and painlessly, provided it is administered at proper injection rates by trained personnel. The report recommends that if barbiturates cannot be used, T-61 appears to be a suitable substitute.

Acceptable

Certain inhalant anesthetics can also provide humane death. Primarily these are ether, halothane and methoxyflurane. The vapors are inhaled until respiration stops and death ensues. There is an advantage to using this inhalant type of euthanizing agent with young or small animals, where giving an injection might prove difficult. Inhalant anesthetics are not usually used in larger animals because of the cost and the difficulty in administration.

A number of other inhalant agents, such as nitrogen, carbon monoxide, hydrogen cyanide or carbon dioxide produce rapid death by producing anoxia. These are frequently used by animal shelters when a large number of animals must undergo euthanasia at the same time. Although these agents are considered painless and effective, the bodily responses they cause in the unconscious animals are aesthetically unpleasant for observers.

Conditional

The AVMA panel on euthansia found certain physical techniques such as rapid decompression, electrocution and shooting acceptable, under certain conditions, for some animals, but not usually for pets. There are many drawbacks to these methods and unless they are properly administered under ideal conditions, the panel found that other means of euthanasia are preferable.

Not Acceptable

Certain methods are considered unacceptable by the AVMA panel. Nicotine is considered dangerous for personnel administering it; chloral hydrate produces objectionable bodily responses in the animals; strychnine is associated with painful reactions before death; magnesium salts used alone have too low a potency to be reliable.

The above material serves as a guide only. A reprint of the full report, which appeared in the July 1, 1978, issue of the *Journal of the American Veterinary Medical Association*, may be obtained by writing to the AVMA (930 Meacham Road, Schaumberg, Illinois 60196). Many owners find it important to approach this subject with as much information as possible in order to hold informed discussions with the veterinarian or animal shelter personnel.

One additional recommendation: if you are planning to use an animal shelter, be certain it is accredited by The Humane Society of the United States, which requires its member agencies to use humane euthanasia methods.

Making the Choice to Participate

Having satisfied yourself that euthanasia is required and that the method will be humane, you may have difficulty deciding whether or not to be present to witness the procedure, or to hold your pet while the lethal dose takes effect. This sensitive matter requires a great deal of thought and should be based on your degree of attachment, emotional strength, and inclination.

Some people prefer to turn the matter over to a professional and retain their memories of a living pet. They may feel that their distress will be overwhelming. Others believe that being present removes the mystery from the procedure, leaving less to the imagination. In a touching article titled "A Death in the Family," which appeared in *The New York Times Magazine*, the late author Judith Wax expressed her feelings about being with her Bedlington terrier, Alfie, until the end:

"Though I sometimes find myself staring at dog-food cans in the supermarket, and my glasses fog up when I hear someone sing, 'What's it all about, Alfie,' I feel O.K. about his death. I know that the shot worked instantly. I saw what became of him, which gives a sort of completion to it. He was a casual type and wouldn't have cared much, but there was even dignity in Alf's departure. And someone who loved him dearly, if a little irrationally, held him until it was over."

From a practical standpoint, being present will assure you that the act was accomplished. Many people fear that their pet will not be put to death humanely as they expect, but will be sent to a medical school or laboratory for experimentation. If you plan to take your pet to an animal shelter, and you do not know the organization's reputation, you can ask to witness the event or view the animal afterward. If you are refused, consider going elsewhere.

Planning Effectively

Since this is probably a pet owner's most difficult time emotionally, schedule the procedure for a time that will produce the least trauma for you. Late in the afternoon, perhaps, when a spouse or friend can be home from work and accompany you. Furthermore, request to be ushered in immediately. One couple who had struggled for months with the decision to euthanize their arthritic, pain-ridden poodle, finally decided they had no choice and planned to bring Beau to the veterinarian's office after regular hours. However, emergency surgery interrupted the veterinarian's schedule that day, and he had to extend his office time by several hours. Unaware of this, the sad couple, carrying Beau, walked into a waiting-room full of people—all of whom seemed to sense their mission. It took a great deal of strength on the part of the couple to remain there. To avoid such an experience, reconfirm your appointment before starting out to insure you will not be kept waiting.

Reactions to Your Loss

Even though you have had a chance to prepare for your loss, you will not miss your pet any the less. With the finality of death comes a deep sense of emptiness and sorrow. However, you may find that some of your grief reactions are more manageable than you expected because you did have advance warning. There is a tendency to start grieving at the first sign of serious illness, so the intensity is diminished by the time death actually occurs. In fact, many people actually feel a sense of relief afterward.

But euthanasia often brings guilt and uncertainty in its aftermath. This is a natural reaction arising from the principle that most of us have been taught since childhood: killing is immoral and the worst act that a human being can commit. Even if you believe that you chose the best option for your cat or dog, investigated every available method, stayed with your pet to the very end, you may still feel that having your pet euthanized was "murder." It is a common feeling; Judith Wax's essay, for example, leads off: "I had Alfie killed not long ago."

Perhaps it is true in the strict sense of the word. But in cases of euthanasia all the facts must be examined. Considerable thought goes into the question: are a few extra months of living worth continued pain and suffering? This may be difficult to answer. If you believe that you have exercised your best judgment in agreeing to euthanasia, then the decision should not be construed as a reason for guilt, but rather as an act of kindness: a loved pet deserves a humane and dignified end to life.

Another cause for guilt is the owner's conviction that euthanasia was an act of selfishness. This can be a misinterpretation of the facts, as illustrated in the following case:

Roland, a single, young, corporate executive, lived with his eight-year-old Malamute, Arno, in a two-family house in suburban Chicago. As the result of a job promotion, Roland was transferred to his company's headquarters in New York City. While his apartment building in Manhattan allowed dogs, Roland found it inconvenient to keep Arno. He was thinking of putting him up for adoption, when his pet developed severe heart disease. The condition required considerable care and expensive medication. Despite Roland's effort, Arno became increasingly ill, and the young man and his veterinarian agreed that the most humane course of action would be euthanasia.

Afterward, Roland found that he missed Arno, yet he also believed he would have more time to devote to his career. Instead, his work began to suffer. He began to sleep poorly. He was depressed, and he found himself only half-listening to his clients. Eventually, Roland consulted a therapist. Exploring his feelings, he began to understand that his depression was largely due to the sense of shame and selfishness he harbored over his part in his dog's death. It took a great deal of time for Roland to conclude that he had based his decision on his pet's crippling illness and not on his own convenience.

An objective look at the facts will often help to resolve guilt in time. Owners are not responsible for their pet's illness. And that is the real, if not direct, cause of death.

The sensitive decision to euthanize your pet takes enormous thought and consideration, and should not be rushed. To arrive at a fair and proper determination, it is necessary to explore all aspects of the matter with your veterinarian. He will guide you, but should not be expected to make the final decision, which must come from you and those close to you. To satisfy yourself that you are doing all you can for your pet, investigate commonly used methods for euthanasia and explore your feelings with your veterinarian. If you have children at home, be as honest as possible about what is happening, and allow them to express their feelings.

If you are so inclined, be with your pet at the end. Your dog or cat knows your touch and will be comforted. Afterward, you may be troubled by guilt as well as genuine sorrow. This is a natural reaction to the taking of life. But allow yourself to deal with the fact that you exercised your best judgment.

6   Putting Your Pet to Rest

Even when a pet's death is expected, there is a natural tendency to avoid dealing with the inevitable. So it is characteristic for many owners to put off thinking about what arrangements should be made for putting the pet to rest. As a consequence, when a pet dies the distracted owner is frequently pressed into making hasty decisions about burial, cremation or other disposal of the body.

Properly laying a pet to rest can contribute greatly to a calm and accepting feeling about the occurrence—a sense of finished business unmarked by lingering regrets. Even children recognize this: as one nine-year-old boy remarked, he "felt better when going to sleep knowing that Sam was comfortable in his special resting place."

This, however, requires that you give thought to what plan is best for your family and in keeping with your beliefs. For many owners, it is very important to know the whereabouts of the pet's remains; others mark the pet's passage from life by scattering its ashes around a favorite spot.

Putting your personal stamp on the arrangements can help remove some of the mystery surrounding death. One pet owner explained it this way: "You may not know what happens in the 'vast forever,' but at least you can be satisfied that you provided your pet with a fitting passage there."

There are several options available for putting a pet to rest, and these are discussed in the following pages, with advice on how to proceed in making the arrangements. In addition, there is a discussion of why many families decide to hold some form of a service to mark a pet's death.

Choosing a Method

Burial

While informal backyard burial is the most common method, some owners use the services of a pet cemetery, which provides individual interment; or a cemetery or animal shelter that arranges communal burial.

Your decision will need to take into account such factors as the availability of land, the local laws governing interment in undesignated places, the accessibility of a pet cemetery and the expense of these different methods.

Proceeding on Your Own

Many people find it extremely satisfying to bury a pet in a familiar yard or field, wrapped in its owner's sweater perhaps, and accompanied by a favorite ball or other plaything. It is a way of returning the animal to nature, and even city dwellers may seek a peaceful spot in nearby countryside, a place that would have appealed to the pet.

The following editorial commentary that appeared some years ago in a Canadian newspaper expresses the meaning and value of burial in a special spot:

Where to Bury A Dog

A subscriber of the Ontario *Argus* has written to the editor asking, "Where shall I bury my dog?"

We would say to the Ontario man that there are various places in which a dog may be buried. We are thinking now of a setter, whose coat was flame in the sunshine, and who, so far as we are aware, never entertained a mean or an unworthy thought. This setter is buried beneath a cherry tree, under four feet of garden loam, and at its proper season the cherry strews petals on the green lawn of his grave. Beneath a cherry tree, or an apple; or any flowering shrub is an excellent place to bury a dog. Beneath such trees, such shrubs, he slept in the drowsy summer, or gnawed at a flavorous bone, or lifted his head to challenge some strange intruder. These are good places in life or in death. Yet it is a small matter, for if the dog be well remembered, if sometimes he leaps through your dreams actual as in life, eyes kindling, laughing, begging, it matters not at all where that dog sleeps. On a hill where the wind is unrebuked, and the trees are roaring, or beside a stream he knew in puppyhood, or somewhere in the flatness of a pasture lane where most exhilarating cattle grazed, is all one to the dog, and all one to you—and nothing is gained, nothing is lost—if memory lives. But there is one place to bury a dog.

If you bury him in this spot, he will come to you when you call—come to you over the grim, dim frontiers of death and down the well-remembered path and to your side again. And though you call a dozen living dogs to heel they shall not growl at him, nor resent his coming, for he belongs there. People may scoff at you who see no lightest blade of grass bent by his footfall, who hear no whimper, people who never really had a dog. Smile at them, for you shall know something that is hidden from them, and which is well worth the knowing. The one best place to bury a good dog is in the heart of his master.

But informal burial requires taking practical matters into consideration. Burying a pet on land that is not designated for that use—even if the land is your own property—may be against the law in your locality. Because it would be impossible to establish control over the depth of such burial plots, and in a shallow site the decomposed remains could be unearthed by children or animals, many local governments forbid interment as a health hazard. If your first choice is informal burial, check with the city clerk or with police to learn what is legal and whether a special permit is required. The grave should be a minimum of three feet deep.

As simple and inexpensive as informal burial may be, it provides no guarantee that the final resting place will remain undisturbed. As land changes hands, the use to which it is put may well change also. Moreover, if your pet dies in winter, the ground you would use for an informal burial may be frozen. Although many veterinarians and animal shelters will hold the pet's body in a vault until the owner is ready to proceed, this long-drawn-out process presents a problem for many people.

Pet Cemeteries

To assure a permanent resting place, immediate burial and perpetual care, many owners turn to a pet cemetery. The services and the atmosphere at these establishments are similar to standard memorial parks. Most contain gardens, lighted walkways, benches and statuary, and furnish an assortment of lined or unlined caskets, and a choice of burial vaults, headstones and monuments. Generally there is a chapel that has private viewing rooms and a specially designated section for a simple prayer service at the time of the burial. Plots are dug in advance, so immediate burial is available.

At the owner's request, cemeteries will place natural or artificial flowers on the grave site, arrange to light reminiscence lamps on special dates and protect the grave with a winter blanket. The pet owner can also subscribe to an endowment plan to provide for perpetual care of the plot— especially important in cemeteries with limited space, because an untended plot might be used again.

Burial in a pet cemetery can cost from $150 to $1550 for the complete interment; caskets alone can range from $40 to $300. The final price depends on the size of the plot, what kind of service is held, the annual care that will be provided and wages in that part of the country.

The concept of a cemetery for pets is not new. The first such establishment in the United States, the Hartsdale Canine Cemetery in Hartsdale, N.Y., dates back to 1896, and is still in existence. More than 40,000 dogs and cats have been buried there over the years. Today there are some 500 pet cemeteries in this country, with the heaviest concentration in the Midwest and Northeast.

Despite the growth of pet cemeteries, their image among the public at large is not always understood or appreciated. Mention of a pet cemetery may be accompanied by negative comments such as the one that appeared in *Newsweek* magazine not long ago. In a review of *Gates of Heaven,* a documentary about a pet cemetery, the critic wrote that the film can "conjure up images of dear departed poodles, weeping ladies in hair curlers and rhinestone glasses, and isn't it all so sad and tacky and vulgar...." In this view, burying one's pet in a cemetery is an act of both poor taste and indulgence on the part of the pampered pet's owner.

But veterinarians, as well as pet-cemetery owners, say this is a one-sided and often unfair view of the phenomenon. The pet cemetery is used by people in all walks of life; what they have in common is that they are compassionate pet lovers. For many, a financial sacrifice is required to afford a memorial for the pet that gave them so much pleasure. If it is an indulgence for some, for others it is a sincere effort toward achieving emotional well-being. A headstone over the grave of a seeing-eye dog, for example, has the message "A Real Angel" inscribed in Braille.

"Lots of people love their animals," said Pat Blosser, executive director of the International Association of Pet Cemeteries near Chicago, "but those that consider their pets total members of the family generally want to provide them with a fitting burial.

"We have a saying here," she added: "People bury people

because they have to, but they bury their pets because they want to."

A young woman whose schnauzer is interred in a memorial park in Pennsylvania explained her motivation this way: "It was a tribute to Missy. She gave me years of pleasure and I owed her something in return. I certainly didn't think of her as a person, but I did consider her a friend."

One of the most comforting aspects of choosing burial in a pet cemetery is that the owner can make periodic visits to the grave site and find a tangible reminder of many happy memories. The value of this, in fact, has recently been recognized in court decisions.

Last year a New York City woman sued and recovered damages from a dog-and-cat hospital for wrongfully disposing of her poodle. According to the court report, the woman had arranged with her veterinarian for the dog to be euthanized and then transported to a pet funeral home. More extravagant than most, she planned an elaborate funeral for the dog, including a headstone, an epitaph and attendance by her two sisters and a friend.

However, as bizarre as the situation may seem, the casket that was delivered to the funeral home contained a dead cat. The owner sued the hospital for mental distress and anguish. Although prior cases had held that a pet is merely an item of personal property and, as such, is worth only its fair market value, the court overruled that precedent. In his decision the judge said: "In ruling that a pet such as a dog is not just a thing I believe the plaintiff is entitled to damages beyond the market value of the dog. A pet is not an inanimate thing that just receives affection; it also returns it." He further noted that a pet "occupies a special place somewhere in between a person and a piece of personal property." The judge found that the owner suffered shock, mental anguish and despondency due to the wrongful destruction of the pet's body and that she was deprived of an elaborate funeral and the right to visit the grave in the years to come. The court awarded her $700 damages, and the decision has since been cited in several other cases.

Communal Burial

For those who cannot afford the cost of a private interment, some cemeteries or shelters will perform a communal burial. While the treatment is obviously not as personal, the arrangement satisfies many owners. The cost varies, depending upon the size of the animal, generally ranging between $15 and $40.

Cremation

An alternative to burial, cremation is becoming more popular and accounts now for nearly 45 percent of pet disposals handled by professional services. It is quick, clean and generally less expensive than burial at a pet cemetery. The choice between private or communal cremation will often depend upon budgetary considerations and whether one wants to retain the pet's ashes.

Individual Cremation

Most pet cemeteries have facilities for performing individual cremation, and will bury the ashes on the grounds or scatter them in special memorial gardens if the owner wishes. Or the ashes can be returned to the owner in an urn or some other specially designed container. It is quite common for owners to bury the ashes in a backyard, scatter them around a pet's favorite spot or preserve them in a special place in the home.

The average charge for individual cremation ranges from about $30 to $80, depending upon the size of the animal, disposition of the ashes and choice of container.

The method has become increasingly popular with pet lovers who move from place to place, because a small urn is easily transported. It is a source of satisfaction for many owners to be able to keep this memorial in their possession.

While it is an efficient and relatively low-cost method, some owners view cremation as a desecration. Some religions forbid cremation, believing it is an act that rejects the tenet of life after death, and many devout people report that they feel uncomfortable using this method for loved pets. One woman expressed her feelings in the following way: "Gretchen was like a member of the family. I wanted to extend my religious views to include her."

Communal Cremation

Some crematoria, animal shelters and veterinarians will perform communal cremation for about $15 or $20. If you think you can be satisfied with this method, in which your pet's ashes are not segregated for purposes of a memorial, it is an economical way for you to handle the matter.

Other Methods

When owners are not concerned about the physical remains of pets, they may turn their animal over to a shelter or a veterinarian for disposal through a sanitation department. There is usually a charge of about $10 for this service.

In some cases, unfeeling owners will simply deposit their pets on a roadside or other unpopulated spot. Compassion aside, this is an abdication of the owner's responsibility to other human beings and to the environment.

Making the Arrangements

Even if your plans have been made in advance, it is wise to contact your veterinarian immediately following your pet's death. He may wish to perform an autopsy to confirm the exact cause of death, especially if he has been treating the animal.

If you are uncertain about procedures to follow in laying

the animal to rest, explore the services your veterinarian provides. Many will make all the arrangements, from picking up the pet at your home to delivering it to a crematorium or pet cemetery. Veterinarians will generally know of the varied services that these establishments offer, and quite often have arrangements with a particular one. If you are undecided, some veterinarians have facilities to store an animal until you make your choice.

Although they will generally charge a small fee for making these arrangements, veterinarians provide support and experience at a distressing time and most people report that they are relieved to turn the matter over to a professional.

A more recent phenomenon is the pet funeral director. He will generally provide the same services as the veterinarian, but will supply transportation, seven days a week around the clock. The costs vary from $50 to $100 for cremation to $100 to $450 for burial. Currently, most of these directors are located in urban areas where disposal is generally more complicated.

The least expensive arrangement, other than proceeding on your own, is to contact an animal shelter. Most will pick up your animal and provide storage until the sanitation department is ready to handle the disposal. The charge is generally around $10.

(It should be noted that charges vary greatly from one establishment to another and that the prices quoted here were accurate at time of publication.)

The Benefits of Holding a Service

No matter what method you choose, offering a simple eulogy at the time of the pet's death provides closure to the event. It is a chance to be involved in the final experience with the pet, to realize the loss and to express feelings about it. The eulogy can be in the form of a letter, a poem, words borrowed from a literary figure whom you admire, or your own thoughts at this time.

The following is a touching farewell to a faithful companion written by Byron in 1808.

Inscription on the Monument of a Newfoundland Dog

Near this spot are deposited the remains of one who possessed Beauty without Vanity, Strength without Insolence, Courage without Ferocity, and all the Virtues of Man, without his Vices. This Praise, which would be unmeaning Flattery if inscribed over human ashes, is but a just tribute to the Memory of Boatswain, a dog.

There are other, simpler ways of saying good-bye that can be very meaningful. The following are examples of eulogies expressed by owners whose pets are buried in the Hartsdale Canine Cemetery:

Four Feet in Heaven
Your favorite chair is vacant now
No eager purrs to greet me
No softly padded paws to run
Ecstatically to meet me

No coaxing rubs, no plaintive cry
Will say it's time for feeding
I've put away your bowl
And all the things you won't be needing

But I will miss you, little friend
For I could never measure
The happiness you brought to me
The comfort and the pleasure

And since God put you here to share
In earthly joy and sorrow
I'm sure there'll be a place for you
In Heaven's bright tomorrow.

Our dear little pal was with us for fourteen years. During that time she proved to be a loyal friend, and on three occasions she saved our lives. This is her reward for her loyalty.

Lonely House

No more cat tracks on the floor
Muddy scratches on the door;

Puffs of hair upon the stairs
Lacy fretwork on the chairs,

Indentations on my bed
Markings where she laid her head,

Smudges on the window pane
Showing where she watched in vain;

Haunts where she is wont to lay
Remind us that she is away.

My house is neater, that is true,
But, oh, so still and empty, too.

A Tribute to a Dog

The one absolutely unselfish friend that man can have in this world, the one that never deserts him, the one that never proves ungrateful or treacherous, is his dog. A man's dog stands by him in prosperity and poverty, in death and sickness. He will sleep on the cold ground when the wintry winds blow and the snow drives fiercely, if only he may be near his master's side. He will kiss the hand that has no food to offer, he will lick the wounds and sores that come in encounters with the roughness of the world. He guards the sleep of his pauper master as if he were a prince. When all other friends desert, he remains. When riches take wings and reputation falls to pieces he is as constant in his love as the sun in its journey through the heavens.

Untitled

And now we lay you down to sleep
You're finally at rest

Our love for you we'll always keep
You were the very best

You gave us joy for thirteen years
A memory for each new day

Then came the day of all my fears
The day you passed away

A part of us you took with you
And I can't stand the pain

But when this life on earth is through
I know we'll meet again.

Children, in particular, benefit from some sort of family service. It allows them to know that their feelings about the pet were shared by others and that the family considered the pet important and worthy enough of a service. Encouraging children to compose their own eulogies affords them the opportunity to take an active part in the event and to express all the things they wanted to say and perhaps never did. Searching for a proper site for the grave or a place to scatter ashes, or selecting a stone or other marker can provide a child a distraction that may be needed at this unsettling time. Sometimes the sheer physical effort of helping to prepare the site can release anxiety and grief.

Involvement in a service can help a youngster gain experience in handling reactions to loss. One mother reported that Bingo's "funeral" was the first one that her ten-year-old son had attended. Jimmy was very attached to his spaniel and he cried openly as the aged dog was laid to rest in the backyard.

Three months later, the youngster's grandmother died. At the funeral, his mother observed that Jimmy wasn't uncomfortable or afraid as children often are. "He knew what we were feeling," she said. "He was not very close to his grandmother—she lived hundreds of miles away—and he didn't pretend to be distressed. But Jimmy understood my husband's grief, because he had suffered a sad loss of his own."

Arranging a proper funeral for a deceased pet can provide a large measure of comfort for a caring owner. As there are a number of ways to proceed with burial or cremation, it is best to think about your preference in advance, when you are under less stress. The method you choose may depend upon your attachment to your pet, the expense involved, local laws governing burial on undesignated land and your religious views, among other variables. Weigh the advantages and disadvantages of each method, but keep in mind your personal preferences. It might seem sensible to arrange for your pet's disposition by one means, but you might feel better using another. Explore the possibilities with your family and consider your friends' experiences. If you are uncertain following your pet's death, contact your veterinarian. He can guide you in a number of matters at this time. Holding a service of even the simplest sort can be of great benefit to children, since it is often their first experience with meaningful loss. It affords them—and you as well—the chance to say to the pet, "You are gone, but not forgotten."

7   Should You Get Another Pet?

Having loved and lost a pet, it is quite natural to think about including another one in your life. Replacement* is a way of filling in the empty spaces, of establishing new ties of affection to substitute for the old. Even those who have other pets at home think of getting another following a loss.

But despite this impulse to fill the void, replacement is not a step that should be taken automatically or hurriedly. In fact, replacement may not be right for you at all. There are many factors that bear consideration, ranging from your feelings about the lost dog or cat, to your lifestyle and your ability to cope with a new animal in your home. Most important is your inclination to accept and provide affection for a new dog or cat, following the loss of a much-loved animal. It requires time and thought to sort out your feelings, to determine when, or if, you and your family are ready to invest emotionally, physically and economically in another pet.

The following pages deal with the indecision that many people face; the factors that induce replacement; why some people replace their pets immediately and some delay; and why others decide irrevocably against replacement. There is also a discussion of pet replacement in anticipation of loss, choosing an appropriate pet, and practical advice in adjusting to the new animal.

---

*In this chapter the word "replacement" is not meant to imply that one pet actually can take the place of another. The concept of replacement, as we use it, refers to the introduction of a new pet into the household following a loss.

ciding About Replacement

Dealing with Your Indecision

Many people waver when it comes to bringing another pet into the house, wanting to recapture their previous enjoyment but concerned about their ability to love the new animal as they did the other. The best advice is to trust your feelings. If you believe you have come to terms with your pet's death, if you seem to be coping with your own sense of loss, if you miss having an animal around, you are probably ready to let a new cat or dog into your life. It may take time to adjust, but the relationship has a good chance for success.

If you had an unusually strong attachment to your pet, you may decide that you cannot accept a substitute, that you have expended all your affection. This is a perfectly natural reaction and an honest appraisal of your feelings and should not be cause for self-reproach. Nor can you be expected to summon up enthusiasm if your family decides to bring in a new pet anyway. The dog or cat may eventually capture your affection, but if it does not, accept your feelings and expect others to respect them as well.

If your decision is at odds with your true feelings, a new relationship may be short-lived. This was the case, for example, for the late Eleanor Perry, the film writer and novelist. Although she had had a very loving and deep attachment to her late poodle Lulu (whom she memorialized in a touching epitaph that appears as an Epilogue to this book), she convinced herself to get another dog "to invest in a new life." She made every effort to establish a bond with her new animal, but the feelings simply weren't there. She recalled, "We tried to live together for a while but eventually I had to find the dog a new home. There was only one Lulu. No other pet could take her place."

Unsuccessful replacement may be disappointing, but it should not be construed as failure. While it is true that you are physically separated from your deceased pet, the emotional bonds are still intact. And it is this continuing attachment—not your lack of ability as a caregiver—that prevents you from establishing a new relationship.

Indecision about replacement also applies to people who have had mixed emotions about pet ownership all along (sometimes without even being aware of it). Perhaps you never wanted a pet at all, but were influenced by other members of your family—a common situation for a parent. You know you will bear the burden of responsibility for the new pet, as you did for the other, yet you are reluctant to deny your children a replacement for a loved cat or dog. Possibly you can resolve your indecision by using the occasion of the new pet's arrival to lay down fresh ground rules for your children about responsibility in caring for the animal.

Sometimes the mixed feelings about replacing a pet stem from the fact that the original pet was a gift, as in the following case: Helen, a middle-aged college professor, did not consider herself a pet lover until she received a kitten from some of her students. Although she never would have acquired a pet by choice, Helen found Snowball to be quite companionable, and they spent eight affectionate years together. When Snowball contracted leukemia and died, Helen began to think about replacement. Her ultimate decision was to forgo getting another kitten, "because it was Snowball I loved, not cats."

In many cases, devoted owners are reluctant to replace their pets because they want to avoid another loss situation. The death of a pet through a tragic accident or euthanasia can leave emotional scars. Similarly, watching a once healthy, frisky pet deteriorate from aging or illness can be painful. But if the remembered joys of pet ownership outweigh, in the end, these disturbing memories and feelings, the chances are that a new cat or dog will eventually find its way into your life.

Occasionally indecision about replacement is due to uncertainty about one's future. If, for example, your children are grown and you are contemplating moving to smaller quarters in a city, it is only sensible to delay a decision. Your new lifestyle may not be conducive to pet ownership, and there is no point in making a commitment that you will regret.

Resolving Your Indecision

Here are some questions worth considering before reaching a decision:

Have you resolved your loss to the point where you are ready to consider a new pet? Or do you feel you will be betraying your dog or cat with a replacement?

Do you think you will be able to treat the new cat or dog as a separate being, or might it remain a shadow of the other pet?

Are your pet-related needs the same now as they were when you first became a pet owner? Did you originally acquire a pet to demonstrate your ability as a responsible caregiver? Or did you want a pet, perhaps, as a child substitute, and now you are ready to have a family?

Do you want to take on the responsibility of a new pet, or would you rather have your freedom for a while?

Do you feel, simply, that your life is empty without a pet?

While it may be difficult to answer some of these questions in advance, thinking about them might give you some indication of your real feelings.

It is also helpful to talk the decision over with others, and when a family is involved, quite necessary. Children should be allowed to express their feelings, for they usually have a vested interest in both the deceased pet and its replacement.

If your family has mixed opinions on replacement, try drawing up a list of advantages and disadvantages that reflect each member's views. Sometimes it is easier to see the situation objectively when all the issues have been committed on paper.

If there is no family involvement, you might want to speak to a close friend, perhaps someone who has undergone a similar experience. Your veterinarian can also be a source of advice. He often deals with this type of situation and might even be able to suggest an appropriate replacement.

But, although many people can give you advice, it must be stressed that the ultimate decision should be determined by your own feelings.

The Decision Against Replacement

Some people know, unquestioningly, that they will not replace their pet. Perhaps they do not want to experience another painful loss, or they may feel that a new animal could never live up to the deceased pet. Their present or future lifestyle may not be appropriate for pet ownership, or economic considerations may come into play—veterinary or kennel fees, food, medication, licensing can strain a budget. It should be stressed that, whatever the reasons, the decision against replacement should not be a cause for guilt. Pet ownership shouldn't be looked upon as a duty, but rather a pleasure. If it's not appropriate for you, accept your decision and enjoy the memories of your former pet.

Deciding in Favor of Replacement

Unless past ownership had negative overtones, one's lifestyle can no longer accommodate an animal, or the emotional investment is now too great, the tendency to want to replace a pet is natural. A pet is a significant presence in most people's lives and its absence leaves an uncomfortable emptiness.

Even when owners delay the decision, most get around to replacing a pet sooner or later. In a random sampling of one hundred people who adopted dogs or cats from the North Shore Animal League, a private shelter outside New York City, only fifteen had never owned pets before. Not all of the remaining eighty-five adopters were reacting to recent pet loss; for some, many years had elapsed since their days of pet ownership. However, the study substantiated findings from veterinarians, breeders and others in animal-related fields, that once having owned a pet, the majority of people tend to acquire another, eventually.

Among the most common motives people give for pet replacement are companionship, affection, security and the need to nurture. In other words, the very reasons that attracted them to pet ownership in the first place. (The many factors contributing to human-pet attachment are discussed in Chapter 1.) One's emotional and physical needs do not disappear, just because a pet died. The pleasure of pet ownership—particularly a longstanding association—leaves its mark; it is natural to want to create a similar relationship.

Sometimes guilt over the death of the pet becomes a motivation for its replacement. If the owner was involved in the pet's accidental death or never resolved his decision in favor of euthanasia, caring for a new pet is a chance to make up for abandoning the other. However, if replacement is based on guilt alone, the relationship may not work out. More constructive motives are generally needed for a successful owner-pet attachment.

Is There a Right Time?

While everyone must move at his own pace, some people do themselves a disservice if they rush out to get a new dog or cat immediately after a pet's death. Some who replace their pets quickly may not have come to grips with separation and loss. Wanting to take their minds off their grief, rather than dealing with it, they believe a new pet will erase the memories of the lost one. This can sometimes lead to difficulty in dealing with the newcomer, a subject that will be discussed later in the chapter.

Sometimes without consulting a child, parents immediately replace a pet, in an attempt to spare the youngster any grief or painful feelings. But too rapid a replacement will deny the child's right to mourn. Youngsters seem to sense this. As one ten-year-old boy expressed it: "If I get a new dog now, that will be unfair to Blackie." Although he looked forward to owning another pet in the future, he felt he would be betraying his pal Blackie to do so right away.

If a child is not allowed to prepare, the new animal may be rejected. This happened when eleven-year-old Nancy was whisked off by her father to buy another puppy the day after her cocker spaniel, Honey, was struck by a car. As a loving parent, he felt he was doing his only child a favor; he was afraid she would be lonely without her pet. But after the first few days, Nancy stopped paying attention to the new puppy, Crumpet, an English spaniel. She was unable to tell her father that she resented the intruder; she was afraid to hurt his feelings, but she also felt disloyal to Honey. So Nancy simply ignored the dog and refused to take any part in his training. A month later the family gave the dog away. Father thought he knew best by providing Nancy with an immediate replacement, but he failed to do the one thing that could have saved the family an unhappy situation. He never asked Nancy whether she was ready for another dog. Had he been more aware of his child's grieving process, he would have allowed her to set her own pace.

There are, however, certain people who do benefit by replacing a pet as quickly as possible, such as owners who live alone and are heavily dependent upon their animals for companionship and participation in life, or childless couples who invest their feelings in a pet as a substitute for children. In such cases, the dynamics of the relationship are not unlike human attachments. When the need is so overwhelming, it might be best to acquire a new pet immediately, although there may be some feelings of unresolved grief to be dealt with at a later time. (As a cautionary note, however, there are some viruses that can linger in a household following the death of an animal from that disease. These include canine distemper, parvo virus, leptospirosis and hepatitis; also feline pneumonitis, calici virus, infectious peritonitis and leukemia virus. If your pet died from any of the above, veterinarians suggest waiting at least one month before introducing a new pet into the household.)

The need to replace a pet immediately also has justification for people with seeing-eye or hearing guide dogs, or in other special circumstances. Their pets serve not only as companions and protectors, but play necessary roles in their daily lives.

This is illustrated in the case of Kenneth, whose struggle with diabetes eventually led to the amputation of both his legs. His dependency on Fritz, a German shepherd, was almost total after he was confined to a wheelchair. The two were alone much of the day until Kenneth's sister returned from work, and Fritz took on many of the roles of a human companion. The young man had occasional visitors because of his mail-order business, and when someone was about to enter the apartment, Fritz added an extra step to his routine. Rather than head for the door as most dogs will, he first ran to Kenneth's room to alert him and then stationed himself behind the wheelchair as if to guide his master. He never left Kenneth's side while anyone was in the house, seeming to sense the young man's helplessness. Brokenhearted after his trusted dog died, Kenneth nevertheless immediately sought to replace him. He realized that practical matters took precedence over his need to resolve the loss.

Barring special circumstances, a good time to think about replacement is when you have put your loss into perspective. Many people are able to resolve their grief within a matter of weeks or months, but for others it may take longer. Just as there is no "right" amount of time to spend on grieving, there is no time limit for replacing a pet. You will know you are ready by your own behavior: your interest in other people's pets may start to increase; you begin to notice pet-sale advertisements; you start making inquiries about the advantages and disadvantages of various breeds. As you focus your attention less and less on the lost pet, you are making room for a new one.

Sometimes this turning point can take years, as it did for animal lover Ellen Popper of New York. Her poodle, Willie, had been with her since she was a young woman, and the bonds of affection between them were extraordinarily strong. The young Ellen took Willie everywhere, including vacations, and even skied with her poodle strapped to her back. The relationship lasted a long time, so long that Ellen had been married for several years at the time of Willie's death. At first she believed she could never replace her beloved little poodle, but she missed having a dog around her. So a few months after Willie's death Ellen arranged to take in a "foster dog," for which she cared until an adoptive family could be found. On the heels of the first dog came another, and then another. In all, Ellen sheltered eighteen dogs and five cats in two years. As a result of her experience in finding homes for her charges, she established the Animal Welfare League of Westchester County (New York), a nonprofit organization that promotes adoption, provides education about pet care and runs a locating service and a clinic.

And, yes, she eventually replaced Willie—three years

later—with two strapping mixed breeds adopted from a shelter. Her situation is hardly typical, but it does indicate that going at one's own pace can bring successful results. There is no need to rush into pet replacement, nor to feel guilty for putting it off.

Replacement in Anticipation of Loss

Some animal lovers feel they cannot live at all without a pet. Consequently, when a dog or cat shows the first signs of illness or aging, they immediately bring in another. This may be due to a healthy realization that a pet's companionship is quite meaningful to them. They want time to establish a relationship with the new animal so it can ease their eventual sense of loss over the other.

However, some people make the acquisition in an attempt to ward off all feelings of separation and loss. This has a way of backfiring. Stifling one's emotions by investing energy and love in another pet does not eliminate grief; it merely pushes it into the background and delays its resolution. The sense of loss may take years to dissipate—or it may never disappear.

Then, too, there may be household conflicts about replacing a pet in advance. What seems like a practical assessment of the pet's condition to some members may appear as abandonment and betrayal to others. These differences need to be worked through before you bring another animal into the house; it is unrealistic to rely on the new pet to charm the reluctant members of the household. Perhaps giving your assurance that the new pet is not taking the other's place, but is a hedge against your expected loneliness, will help others in your family to understand that you are not being disloyal.

If you do decide to bring in a new animal, consider how your sick or aged pet will receive the newcomer. Since a new pet can be intrusive and very threatening, it is wise to provide as much attention as possible to the established pet.

In the book *The Inner Cat: A New A*
havior, the author, Carole Weilbourn,
"Introducing New Feline Members
Among her sensible recommendations: the p
not be the one to arrive with the new animal.
"You cannot just bring the newcomer in, plop him dow
front of your cat and expect them to be off to a perfect
start." She suggests that a "neutral party" bring in the new
animal and that in the beginning the owner be "oblivious to
the new arrival even if he's staring you in the face." This
book and others on animal behavior will guide you in introducing the new cat or dog.

Some people take in additional pets simply because they
like having more than one. But if the pet is to be an advance
replacement, make sure that you really want it, that you are
ready to take on the added responsibility, that you do not
feel pressured into the acquisition and that you have enough
affection for both the new and the old.

What Type of Pet Should You Get?

Selecting the most suitable replacement pet is certainly worthy of as much consideration as you gave to acquiring your
first pet. Your age and lifestyle, the ages of your children,
your living conditions and your personal preferences are all
likely to influence your decision.

While many experienced pet owners enter into replacement knowing exactly what type of pet they want, others are
uncertain. The question that arises most frequently is whether to replace with the same breed. Sometimes owners feel
that getting the same breed is, in fact, getting the same dog.
If that is your wish, you may be leaving yourself open to
disappointment. Although the two pets may share many of
the same characteristics, every animal has a personality of its
own. You might spend a great deal of emotional energy com-

...g the two, rather than enjoying the new dog or cat for ...lf. However, if you are willing to acknowledge the differ-...ce between the two animals, you will probably find it easi-er and more predictable to deal with the same breed.

Some people use replacement as an opportunity to switch to another breed, to a pet of a different size or temperament. The change can be enjoyable, providing the choice is appro-priate. But certain breeds are simply ill-suited to certain pro-spective owners, as in the following case:

An elderly couple, apartment dwellers, went to an animal shelter in New York to adopt a pet following the death of their Scottie. After some deliberation they selected a frisky young German shepherd. It was obvious to the staff that this was a poor choice; the animal would require a great deal of exercise and space. However, the couple insisted upon taking the dog home, for it reminded the man of a pet he had owned as a youngster in Germany. Within a few days the couple returned with the young shepherd. To everyone's re-lief, they chose instead a small terrier mix that was older, more sedate and more manageable. (This solution raises a point. Shelters have literally millions of mature animals al-most impossible to adopt out. The elderly are often afraid to get pets because they cannot meet the demands of caring for a young animal. The mature animal can make a perfect "in-stant pet" for aging individuals.)

To avoid mistakes it is advisable to weigh the advantages and disadvantages of the breeds you are considering in ad-vance. Dogs or cats that look "cute" in a pet store or kennel are tempting, but they may not have the characteristics you want. Discuss various breeds with breeders, kennel and pet store owners, veterinarians and friends. Relate the size and temperament of the breed to your personal living conditions, the ages of your children, the amount of exercise you are willing to provide, and the frequency of grooming. Think, too, of the small things: will you mind light-colored fur shedding on your dark rugs or furniture, for example?

While a number of people experiment with a different breed, the majority stay loyal to the species. But there can be good reasons for changing. A cat lover may decide to acquire a dog if there are children in the house who want a more active animal, or if the family wants protection. And many former dog owners decide that although they want another pet, they also want to simplify their lives. A cat is easier to care for and provides a quieter kind of relationship. Switching from one species to another is a big change, almost like starting over. While your experience as a pet owner will be helpful, you might consider consulting your veterinarian or any one of a number of books on the care and upbringing of your new pet.

When deciding how old an animal to bring home, many people are swayed by the appeal of a puppy or kitten. There is no denying the pleasure these little balls of fluff bring, or the satisfaction one has in raising a pet from infancy. However, young animals require a great deal of effort, even from experienced pet owners. The responsibility for feeding, training, frequent visits to the veterinarian and, in the case of dogs, walking and cleaning up after "accidents" should not be overlooked or minimized.

On the other hand, although an older cat or dog has certain advantages brought about by maturity, you must be willing to accept that it has been raised and trained by others.

Adjusting to Your New Pet

The first one to three months with your new animal is an important time psychologically. Many people assume that things will be the same as they were before the loss; that the animal will respond to the same phrases, commands, gestures, and even tones of voice as did the other; that the same pet food, games and toys will entice. When this fails to happen, it can lead to disappointment or even anger at the new animal. Without the understanding that their anger may be due to unrealistic expectations, many owners will simply give up and return the cat or dog. Some may try again with a different breed, but successful replacement may still be impossible if they are longing for a carbon copy of the lost pet.

Sometimes a new pet will develop a habit or attitude that reminds you of your other animal, and in the process reactivate your original feeling of loss. This is a normal reaction; deal with it by acknowledging the similarity and the memories it evokes. Eventually you will find that the gesture has more association with the new pet than the old.

Some Guidelines for Adjustment

The following advice may help smooth the way for a successful beginning with your new pet:

Remember that the decision to take in another pet in no way shows disloyalty or disregard for the other cat or dog. In fact, it can be a reaffirmation of the good relationship you once had; you are trying to create another.

Acknowledge that you have a stranger in your home. Don't expect an instant "member of the family," particularly if the replacement follows the loss immediately.

Leave yourself time to adjust. If possible, make plans to bring the new pet home when you can give some unhurried attention to its training and other needs. A long weekend or a vacation from work would be an ideal time.

Try not to expect your new dog or cat to act like its predecessor. Every animal has its own distinctive characteristics and personality traits. Look for them, and you probably will find some delightful differences. Some people give the animal the same name as the other. This can be counter-productive, impeding the full realization of the first pet's death. While comparisons are inevitable, the sooner you accept the new pet for itself, the sooner you will be building a healthy relationship.

Allow yourself to think about the deceased pet; it takes less emotional energy to express these feelings than to stifle them. In all likelihood these thoughts will diminish as the new pet works its way into your life. However, if you find that the animal simply cannot take the other's place, you may need to consider finding a new home for it. This is understandable and should not be looked upon as a sign of failure. To the contrary, it shows intelligence to know when to end a situation.

Just as you give yourself time to adjust, respect the right of other family members to accept at their own pace. Not everyone will take to the new pet in the same way or at the same speed.

While it is natural to want to replace a significant loss, taking in a new pet is a large commitment that requires considerable reflection. For some people the decision is easy: they have no hesitation about their desire for a new pet and may even have selected the breed and the name before losing their original pet. Others know, unequivocally, they will never own another pet, for they care to make neither the physical nor the emotional investment.

But if you are uncertain, even after weighing all the advantages and disadvantages, then you are probably not ready. Take your time and accept your indecision, knowing it will resolve itself eventually.

There is no rule of thumb as to how much time should elapse before replacing your pet: it can take days, weeks, months or years. You will know when you are ready for another pet when life for you or your family seems empty without one. Nor is there a blueprint defining the type of animal you should get. A range of factors, from your personal preferences to your present and future way of life, are all part of the decision.

Successful pet replacement requires not only a desire to fill a void but a willingness to invest physical energy and love in the new animal. It also involves a readiness to accept the loss of the other, and to think of the new pet as a wholly separate being. It is worth the effort to gather information for an intelligent decision—your pet will be with you for a long time.

8   Loss Unrelated to Death

Before Ralph and Betty moved into their apartment with their Irish wolfhound, Sean, the landlord assured them that he would overlook the clause in the lease prohibiting pets. Six months later the building was sold and the new owner notified the tenants that they had a choice: get rid of their pets or move.

Daniel went shopping with his poodle, Dapper, and left him in the car while he made a brief stop at the market. When he returned, Dapper was gone, a petnapping victim.

Linda, a thirty-two-year-old teacher, developed severe allergies to her Maltese cat's dander. Her frequent asthma attacks forced her to realize she could no longer keep Muffin.

When Carol opened the door to get her mail, Sesame, her greyhound, darted out. When the dog failed to return after three days, Carol realized that she might never see Sesame again.

These are examples of pet loss that is unrelated to death, but just as capable of disrupting an owner's life, sometimes quite unexpectedly. It is often as hard on people who lose living pets as it is for those grieving for loved animals that have died. The interruption in the relationship can bring about the same feelings of bereavement and emptiness and may well trigger anger and guilt over the unfair circumstances surrounding the loss.

This kind of loss can be divided into two categories: voluntary separation, where there is a certain amount of choice and control over the decision; and involuntary separation, where the pet is missing or develops behavioral problems (such as a tendency to bite) and must be given up. In the following pages, a discussion of some of the circumstances that lead to such separations offers advice on dealing with the different situations, information on settling a pet into a new environment and strategies for recovering a lost or stolen animal.

Voluntary Separation

The expression "voluntary separation" is misleading in a way, because it implies that one is willing to give up the pet. While it is true that a choice is involved, many owners part with their pets reluctantly, pushed into the decision by outside circumstances. This type of loss is often accompanied by guilt as well. The person who develops allergies, for example, or whose promotion requires moving and leaving the pet, feels responsible to the entire household for the loss. There is also a great deal of anger; one naturally resents being forced into a difficult choice between a pet and some other desirable object or goal.

However, in voluntary separation there are benefits that often can offset painful loss reactions. A newly married pet owner whose partner doesn't appreciate sharing the bed with a dog or cat may be inclined to give up the pet rather than the marriage. The pet will no doubt be missed, but there is the plus of marital accord to diminish the sense of loss.

The following are some common situations which lead people to give up pets voluntarily:

Allergic Reactions

One of the most common causes for pet-owner separation is the allergic reaction triggered by the cat or dog. The onset can be sudden. With no previous history of symptoms, one can develop itchy eyes, a runny nose, sneezing spells, difficulty in breathing or other respiratory problems. A rash or hives may also develop. The decision to relinquish your pet may depend upon the frequency or severity of your symptoms, the advice of your allergist, and how well you can function under the circumstances.

The following is typical of the cases that allergists see:

At the urging of their ten-year-old son, Andy, the Johnson family acquired a sheepdog puppy from a neighbor's litter. For three years the young boy shouldered the responsibility of caring for, training and grooming the big shaggy dog, and Ben showed his trust by lumbering up on Andy's bed each night and sleeping with his friend. Then, at age thirteen, Andy developed frequent bouts of wheezing. His labored breathing sidelined him from sports and occasionally kept him home from school. An allergist's evaluation indicated that Andy was allergic to the dander of dogs. When allergy shots failed to relieve his symptoms, the doctor recommended that Ben be removed from the house.

During the next few weeks the family debated putting up Ben for adoption. The discussions began with a logical look at the facts and ended in lost tempers and tears. At one point Andy stubbornly declared that he and Ben would go away together, he did not care how sick he felt. But after a particularly severe attack, the youngster was persuaded to relinquish his pet.

The separation was painful. Andy felt the loss intensely and resented his own body for betraying him. He spent a listless summer without Ben, but in the fall, when he made the junior varsity basketball team, he began to appreciate the changes his dog's absence had made in his life.

This example demonstrates the double bind that often accompanies giving up a pet. Andy's parents were torn between doing what was right for their son's health and feelings of guilt about separating him from his trusted friend. Andy, struggling with the anticipated loss of his cherished dog, was unable to appreciate the rationale for parting with him. He viewed his parents' stand as negative and arbitrary, choosing to ignore the reality of his symptoms and the benefits that could be gained from giving up his pet.

When dealing with children in these situations, it is important to allow them time to accept the inevitable. When a child has a chance to become accustomed to the separation and to say good-bye, the loss may be resolved more quickly.

Some allergists (but certainly not all) believe that desensitization may help in some cases, and they recommend that certain measures be taken before the pet is given up. For example, an owner might try reducing the amount of fabric in the house, substituting tile floors for carpeting, using non-pile furniture covering, blinds instead of drapes, putting laundry bleach in the pet's bath, or keeping the animal outside. While there is no guarantee that these steps will eliminate the allergy, some owners and allergists feel that they are worth trying.

Lifestyle Changes

Many people choose to give up a pet because they perceive the dog or cat as an obstacle to a desirable new way of life.

The prospect of relocating to a foreign city, the impending arrival of a new infant in the home or the desire to move to a smaller apartment after grown children have left the house are typical of lifestyle shifts that can cause one to reevaluate present pet ownership.

Should you arrange to transport a pet four thousand miles? Is it worth the expense?

Is it a risk to keep a large dog in the same home as a helpless infant? Can you be certain that the dog will never turn on the child?

In searching for living quarters, should you be limited to only those spaces that allow animals? Would the pet adjust to a small apartment, after having the run of a house and yard?

After weighing the answers to questions like these, you may decide that giving up your pet is the best course for all concerned. While some people make the choice and are relatively untouched emotionally, you may find it a difficult tradeoff. Although logic dictates your decision, your strong connection to the pet does not dissolve overnight. Stifling your feelings by telling yourself how lucky you are in your new circumstances will only prolong your distress. It is natural to miss your pet, so accept your feelings.

Sometimes one must shift pet ownership, as the result of divorce or other broken relationship. The decision about who keeps the cat or dog has been the basis for many a custody fight, and visitation rights are often part of the negotiations. However, the arrangement may backfire if the partner keeping the animal concludes that ownership is incompatible with an unattached lifestyle.

This was the position in which Terry, a twenty-eight-year-old medical secretary, found herself. Six months earlier she and Angelo had signed a separation agreement, giving her custody of Bruno, their five-year-old Labrador mix, in exchange for his keeping their valuable record collection. Terry was convinced that she came out the winner—an assortment of inanimate discs was no match for a loving dog. But of course Bruno required attention, and Terry gradually began to resent having to schedule her social life around her pet. She also was somewhat fearful of walking Bruno alone at night.

Just as she regretfully concluded she had made a mistake in keeping him, she heard about a newly married couple looking for an older dog. Bruno fitted their specifications exactly: he was housebroken, accustomed to being alone during the day and had a gentle, playful disposition.

Buyer and seller planned to meet, with the stipulation that

if either side was dissatisfied there would be no exchange. Terry arrived at the Coopers' home with Bruno, his toys, feeding dishes, leash, and a couple of pictures of him as a puppy. After providing information about her pet's habits and dealing with the young couple's questions, Terry prepared to leave—in tears. No one ever said it was easy to give up a pet.

After his former owner departed, Bruno stayed by the door for the rest of the evening; he continued his patrol, on and off, for a day or so more. During the next two weeks Terry called the Coopers several times; she was prepared to find Bruno another home if the arrangement was unsuccessful. Eventually, Bruno became adjusted to his surroundings and his new owners consider him a member of the family.

While Terry was honest with herself about resenting Bruno, she felt responsible for placing her pet with suitable owners. By meeting and keeping in touch with them, she satisfied herself that her former pet was being well cared for.

Career Demands

Having to choose between a pet and a career can be particularly divisive. Most people really want both, and resent having to make the choice. In general, however, a meaningful job opportunity can be a powerful incentive, strong enough to induce many to sacrifice ownership and attachment to a loved pet. The following vignette is presented as an illustration:

Three years ago, when Shelby was promoted to personnel manager in a branch office of a major airline, her ambitions were well satisfied: the change brought increased salary, responsibility and prestige. She worked hard and, after eight months, was asked to spend extended periods of time overseeing operations at other offices in this country and abroad.

The job, with its new travel demands, would require her to

give up Baccarat, her four-year-old Angora. It took Shelby several days to establish her priorities. She struggled with feelings of selfishness and disloyalty, but eventually concluded that her job had to come first. Unable to find a suitable home for Baccarat before her first travel assignment, she boarded the cat at her accustomed kennel. By the time she returned, the kennel owners had located a family interested in adopting the Angora.

Shelby's situation exemplifies what increasing numbers of single people have to face regarding their careers. With people marrying later, career choices are becoming more critical than ever. If you are confronted with this type of decision, focus on whether it is career advancement or continued pet ownership that will do more to enhance your well-being—both now and in the future.

Housing Priorities: No Pets Allowed

Throughout the country there are apartment houses and other multiple dwellings that prohibit animals. Dog and cat lovers generally avoid these premises when hunting for a home, assuming they can find suitable quarters where their pets are welcome. Sometimes, however, they find space where landlords will grant consent even if there is a lease clause to the contrary. And in these situations, the pet will have a home at least until the expiration of the lease, as long as it is not a nuisance. When the new lease is negotiated, the pet once again may be forced to pass the landlord's admission test. But pet owners who live in these places often have advance warning if the management is planning a change of heart.

When a tenant under lease does not have the landlord's consent in writing, a change of position by the landlord could result in a court battle. The outcome would depend upon whether the judge concluded that fairness ("equity") toward the tenant overrode the legal dictates of the written lease.

The tenant who loses the case or cannot afford the cost of the lawsuit is forced into a difficult choice: move or lose a pet. If you find yourself in this situation, either alternative can cause a serious upheaval in your life.

Choosing to part with your pet can result in depression, anxiety and grief reactions. Your feelings may be reminiscent of earlier confrontations with authority; as a child you lacked control and the ability to alter a situation. You may experience the same sense of frustration and helplessness now. The best advice is to find a suitable adoptive home for your pet and deal with the reality that your situation was tenuous. Initially, you may have hoped that the living arrangements would work out, but there were no guarantees.

Moving to suitable living quarters and keeping your cat or dog is the best course of action, but it is often easier said than done. If you are lucky enough to find new space, examine the lease carefully and save yourself a similar upheaval in the future.

Economic Considerations

The cost of keeping a pet is not traditionally considered a large item in the budget of an active wage earner. But those on fixed incomes often must make sacrifices in order to own their pets. A cat or dog requiring surgery, for example, may cost its owner $300 or $400 for hospitalization, veterinarian's fees and medication, before fully recovering. This is in addition to expenses for food, standard veterinary visits and other customary costs. Sometimes these expenses prove to be unmanageable, as in the following case:

Having to depend upon Social Security benefits for all of her needs, Sara was finding it difficult to support herself. The seventy-five-year-old widow lived a meager existence in a one-room apartment, allowing herself only two luxuries—her cats Abby and Tiffany. When the landlord raised the rent, Sara could no longer pay for cat food. There was no other solution but to bring her pets to an animal shelter. The manager there reassured Sara that until they were adopted, she could visit her cats whenever she wished. While the arrangement was a poor substitute for ownership, Sara knew that she had no choice, for she had no other way of providing for herself.

Sara's predicament is an increasingly common one. Many aging people on fixed incomes are unable to support themselves and their pets at the same time. And for many of these older citizens, their pets are their only companions. The loss of these animals may account for a number of reactions: increased isolation, reliving of previous losses, depression, and feelings of anger because there is little control over the economic situation. To deal with these feelings, you should recognize the absolute necessity of your action. You had no choice; your physical well-being depended upon giving up your pet.

Destructive Pets

People occasionally believe they can no longer keep a pet that is destroying their belongings because the behavior is uncorrectable. In reality, they may not be exploring ways of improving the situation because they want to rid themselves of the animal for other reasons. The following story is presented to illustrate this point:

Eileen is a forty-three-year-old divorced mother of three sons, aged sixteen, twelve and ten. A year ago the family acquired a collie mix, but now Eileen wants to put up the dog for adoption because she says it is untrainable. The dog has eaten through a sofa, two chairs, the rugs in three rooms and almost all the wires in the apartment. She describes the dog as spoiled ("thinks he's a prince") and says that she is tired of the responsibility. She also complains that the dog eats only expensive food and that she is going into debt.

Eileen recently obtained a loan to buy new rugs and plans to give up the dog when the new items arrive. Her sons threaten to run away if she carries out the plan. She, in turn, claims that the boys take no responsibility for their pet, and this increases her anger and resentment. Despite her feelings, she continues to buy expensive dog food and toys. During the course of several psychotherapy sessions, it became apparent that Eileen had hidden motives for giving up the pet. The dog represented a way of controlling her children: by getting rid of him she could retaliate against her sons' irresponsibility. It was an assertive action, a move calculated to strengthen her position as a mother. She made no effort to train the dog; if it behaved she would no longer have a hold over her sons.

The therapist suggested that she consult an animal behaviorist who could help improve the pet's behavior. Presumably that would improve matters in the household. If the plan failed Eileen then would consider putting up the pet for adoption.

When giving up your pet, examine your motives carefully. You will make the transition from owner to nonowner more smoothly if you genuinely believe that you acted in your own and your family's best behalf.

Finding a New Home for Your Pet

One of the best ways to make yourself feel more at ease about giving up your pet is to locate a suitable new home and caring owners for the animal. The following guide is designed to assist you in placing your pet satisfactorily. The suggestions are listed in order of preference:

1. Find a friend or relative who knows the animal and is willing to give it a home. Never give your pet to a reluctant taker; there is a chance that the new owner will pass it on, setting off a chain reaction. Too many owners in a short time can traumatize an animal, making it an unsuitable pet.

2. Ask your veterinarian for names of prospective owners. Practitioners often have clients looking for second pets or replacements following loss. There is a good chance that your veterinarian will know something of the individual's background as it relates to responsible pet ownership.

3. Find an adoption service with a solid reputation and a high rate of placement. These organizations may be located through your veterinarian or animal shelter. Although many do not have facilities to shelter pets, they serve as clearinghouses, matching people with animals.

4. Try to find an adoptive home on your own, by asking for leads from friends or relatives, or by advertising in a newspaper. When you are considering placing your cat or dog with a stranger, try to visit the home where your pet will be living. If that is impossible, meet the prospective owners before you make any firm commitment, and try to gauge their attitudes by how they act with both you and your dog or cat. If you feel uncomfortable handing over your pet, trust your judgment. Think the matter through carefully before making a final decision. It is a long-term commitment.

5. A good, but costly, solution for an older, less adoptable pet is a retirement home, where a cat or dog can live uncaged with other animals for the rest of its life. The residence is generally a private house acquired specifically for the purpose and run by "foster parents." One of the first established in the country, the Kent Retirement Home in Suffolk County, New York, charges $3,500 for a cat and $6,500 for a dog, which includes expenses for the life of the pet.

Since this is a new concept in pet care, there are still very few retirement homes in the United States. Information may be obtained from veterinarians, adoption services, Societies for the Prevention of Cruelty to Animals, or The Humane Society of the United States. A word of caution: visit the home and check the conditions before you turn your pet over for life. Not every retirement-home owner has the same standards.

6. Take your pet to a shelter, but first investigate its reputation by calling The Humane Society of the United States in Washington, D.C. (202-452-1100), which has a local society accreditation service. Find out how long the shelter will hold the pet, what the adoption policies are and the manner in which pets are euthanized if not adopted.

7. Finally, you may decide to have your pet euthanized. If an animal has little chance for adoption, many pet-care specialists recommend considering this procedure. According to a representative of The Humane Society of the United States, providing a humane death may be superior to adopting out a pet that will be confined for the rest of its life. Experts believe that a pet that has known home life becomes traumatized and unadoptable after it has been confined for a period of time. If you think that your pet will be unadoptable, you may want to talk over this alternative with your veterinarian.

If you must give up your pet by a certain time, do not wait until the last minute to start making arrangements. If necessary, board the animal until you are satisfied that you can place it in a suitable new environment.

Be aware that there are people who acquire pets for conversion into "cellar" or watchdogs, for experimentation or worse. If you care about your pet's fate, investigate the prospective owner's background and motivation carefully.

After finding a home, leave your telephone number with the new owner. If the adoption is unsuccessful, don't just walk away from the situation. Ask to be informed so that you can make other arrangements. It is your obligation as the original owner to be responsible for your pet's future. Check in with the new owners periodically to answer any questions about your pet's habits.

Involuntary Separation

There are certain non-death-related losses over which an owner has no control: when a pet disappears or when it must be sent away because it is designated as a dangerous animal. Unlike voluntary separation, which is a tradeoff of sorts—your health or career, for example, in exchange for your pet—there are few benefits to be gained from an unwilling parting.

The Missing Pet

When a cat or dog disappears, there is bound to be more than a sense of loss. Adding to the emptiness is the mystery of the animal's whereabouts. When dealing with the unknown, it is an unfortunate fact of human nature that we imagine the worst. While it is possible that the animal is perfectly safe, there is no assurance to that effect. Therefore, we tend to conjure up visions of a hungry and homeless pet, a serious accident or worse. We may not even know whether the pet ran away of its own volition or was stolen.

A common misconception is that some pets disappear because they are going off to die. However, according to Dr. Randi Lockwood, an animal behaviorist at the State University of New York, there is no scientific evidence to link a domesticated animal's disappearance with its impending death. When they are ill or injured, pets have an awareness that something is wrong and consequently they prefer to be by themselves. Perhaps it is this need for isolation that leads them away from the household, giving owners the impression that they are wandering off to a peaceful death.

When a pet disappears it is characteristic for woebegone owners to search—hopefully viewing any pet that bears the slightest resemblance to the missing animal as their own lost dog or cat. The searching continues for a long time, possibly even years, and may occur after the pet has been replaced. It is a natural response that allows people to feel they are putting forth effort to recover their pets.

The Runaway

This type of loss is often accompanied by guilt on the part of the person who left the pet unattended. In many cases the feeling is justified; a pet's reliability for staying close to home should not be taken for granted. Accepting the responsibility is a way of coming to terms with the guilt.

One also may be angry—at the pet for running away or at the individual who allowed it to run loose. While your anger may be legitimate, keep in mind that whoever let the pet out might have been following a long-established household pattern. Be fair in your criticism; if it was a family habit to allow the pet loose every day, then everyone is equally responsible for the loss.

The following advice is designed to help you deal with your feelings over the missing cat or dog:

1. Don't waste your anger at your dog or cat for leaving. Animals act impulsively. When they wander off they don't "intend" not returning. Animals simply do not have the ability to project ahead and anticipate the results of an action.

2. On the other hand, express your anger in a reasonable way to the person you believe was responsible for letting the pet loose. It will clear the air and will allow you to feel less helpless.

3. Accept the responsibility for your negligence, if you feel you were at fault. But don't shoulder an unfair burden of guilt. If you were away and the babysitter allowed the pet to run out, for example, it makes no sense to blame your vacation, unless, of course, you failed to leave proper instructions.

4. Make every effort to find your pet. Don't sit by passively

and expect it to return, for it may not. (Suggestions for locating a missing pet are outlined later in this chapter.)

5. Accept your sense of loss and allow yourself to grieve. Be prepared to ignore insensitive friends who tell you a missing animal isn't worth your tears.

6. After a reasonable amount of time—one or two months—accept the fact that your pet is gone. Your dog or cat may turn up later, and that is a bonus. Meanwhile, set yourself a time limit and then start thinking about replacement. This will allow you to close the file on your missing pet—although you might find that you are still searching occasionally.

The Stolen Pet

In general, the same feelings and advice will apply when a pet is stolen. However, the anger and guilt often are more exaggerated. The willful violation of personal property brings about enormous—and legitimate—hostility, yet there is usually no known thief upon whom to vent these feelings. Guilt and self-reproach may be intensified—for allowing a helpless animal to be spirited away, for failing to protect a cherished belonging. These exaggerated feelings often heighten one's grief reactions, as in the following case:

In a departure from her normal routine, Kate, a systems analyst, left her Doberman pinscher, Astrid, leashed to a parking meter in Manhattan, while she ran an errand in a neighborhood store. She hurried the clerk along, feeling uneasy about leaving the animal untended—and her premonition was correct. When she stepped outside, Astrid was gone.

Kate, who lived alone, spent the next three months searching for her pet. She called the police, put up posters and spent hours tracking down leads. She found that she had to protect herself against the many cranks who tried to give her false information about Astrid's whereabouts.

Throughout the ordeal, one thought kept recurring: "What are they doing to my girl?" Her initial reaction of shock and disbelief eventually gave way to depression. She found herself unable to concentrate on her work, instead focusing most of her energies on the missing pet. After a while she received very little support from her friends, who became impatient with her singleminded "obsession."

After three months she conceded that she would never see her pet again. She bought another Doberman, a mature dog with a remarkable resemblance to Astrid. Walking with Saturn one afternoon a month later, she was approached by a youngster who asked if the dog belonged to the same litter as the Doberman he had just seen a few streets away near his school. Kate fairly flew through the neighborhood with Saturn, hoping to catch sight of this "twin." Like a storybook ending, it turned out to be Astrid, living, ironically, less than a mile away from her old home. Although they believed they had obtained Astrid legitimately, the family eventually returned the dog to Kate after she positively established her original ownership.

Kate had great luck recovering her pet. However, not many petnappings have such happy endings. It is worth the effort to keep a watchful eye on an animal you love if you want to avoid a traumatic experience of this type.

If Your Pet Disappears

The following suggestions are adapted from the book *Sherlock Bones*, by John Keane, a professional tracer of lost pets. The original, more detailed material may be found in the chapter "How to Find Your Missing Pet."

1. Call your animal shelter, police department and emergency after-hours veterinary hospitals. You should act immediately if any of these places say they have your pet. A delay in picking up the animal may result in its being mistakenly destroyed. If the police or shelter claim not to have your pet, it is worth stopping by anyway, because telephone descriptions can be misinterpreted.

2. Determine a reward. This is an important part of the search procedure because it may induce someone who is keeping your pet to give it up. Depending upon the value you place on the animal, the reward should range between $50 and $300. A good rule of thumb: $50 for an average-looking mixed-breed dog; $100 for a pure-bred; $300 for an outstanding animal. Of course, this depends upon your budget as well, but the more substantial the reward, the better chance you have of retrieving your animal.

3. Design a poster. Use standard- or legal-size paper (big enough to be noticed, small enough not to clutter store windows, causing merchants to object). Include the following: your telephone number, but not your name and address; the pet's name; the vicinity where the pet was lost; the day, date and time of the loss; a brief description including color, identifying marks and size in weight; whether or not your pet was wearing tags (you might add "possibly," because they may have been removed); and if medication is needed, include the name, dosage and symptoms that might occur without it. You can hand-letter the poster but it is more eye-catching if you have it prepared by a typesetter.

4. Have a thousand copies of your poster printed. This can be done at a copy center or instant printer for about $20. If you plan to use a picture (which, incidentally, should be taken at various stages of a pet's development and which should exhibit clearly all markings and identification points), discuss the technical aspects with the printer, as he cannot work directly from a photograph. Use white paper for the background; it will stand out.

5. Visit all shelters in your area. Plan on going every other day if possible, depending upon your schedule and how long the animals are held. Visit all the rooms where the animals are kept, including the quarantine area. Check lost-and-found lists (some people report a found pet but don't bring it to the shelter); check records of pets under both male and female listings (shelter personnel can make mistakes); check the cat cages for a small dog if the shelter is overcrowded; display your poster on the bulletin board of the shelter.

6. Distribute the posters. Since many animals are found close to where they were lost, concentrate posters in an area 20 blocks from your home (or neighborhood where the pet disappeared) in all directions. Include your old neighborhood if you just moved, and schools or shopping centers just outside the twenty-block area. Staple posters to telephone and utility poles at low eye level to make them visible for pedestrians and motorists alike. Put them on poles near gathering places: bus stops, schools, playgrounds, recreational facilities; in high-traffic, long-hour stores like supermarkets, laundromats. Place posters in veterinarians' offices, with groomers, kennels and other animal-related facilities. Alert people who make rounds, such as postmen, milkmen, newspaper deliverers, sanitation men. And remember to remove the posters when your search is over.

7. Run newspaper ads. A sample might include information on the reward; the pet's name; a physical description; a description of the collar; day, date and time lost; vicinity where lost; your telephone number (but not your name or address). Read the lost-and-found ads as well—someone may be looking for *you*.

8. Wait for the leads to come in. Make yourself available at the telephone. Try to get the caller's name and address first and then ask for the information. Let the caller supply the description; if you ask leading questions, you might get answers you want to hear—but they may be inaccurate. If you think it is a crank call, get the telephone number and call back.

9. Try some "positive-imaging." Listen to and act on your intuitive feelings about where your pet might be, where to put up a poster, whom to talk to. This may not be a "scientific" approach but it is more effective than many people realize.

10. Exercise caution and common sense when recovering your pet. Arrange to meet at the person's home, or if you are suspicious make it a public place or stay inside your car. It is also wise to bring along a friend. Pay the reward in cash or cashier's check, not with a personal check that can identify you. Do not pay until you have the pet in your possession.

Separation from a Harmful Animal

While laws vary throughout the country, many municipalities direct that if a dog is known to have bitten or attacked people, or is examined by a veterinarian and found to be vicious, it is ordered destroyed or restrained. Some domesticated dogs may turn harmful when hungry or provoked or when protecting their owners or territory. It matters little under the law what the circumstances are; the courts will not allow a dog with a reported history of biting to be kept as a pet.

Some owners, recognizing that their dogs have a propensity for dangerous behavior, will act before the courts do. They are aware that keeping a vicious dog is a liability like keeping a hazardous substance. Rather than risk a pet's doing further injury and having to be destroyed, they will arrange to place the animal in a different environment—to be retrained as a guard dog or watchdog, perhaps. Another possible solution is to consult a professional trainer or animal behaviorist. These specialists are trained to deal with behavioral control; in many cases they are able to work with animals to help them "unlearn" their negative behavior. If, however, the dangerous tendencies cannot be controlled or eradicated, the owner is well advised to surrender the animal.

Unfortunately, there are many people who prefer to ignore their dog's dangerous tendencies. In New York City alone, there are 15,000 reported dog bites each year, according to the city's Department of Health. And it is believed that at least 15,000 more go unreported. Of those that are reported, 90 percent are attributed to owned dogs, indicating that vicious behavior may reflect improper handling and training.

The fact that a dog is sent away because of dangerous tendencies does not make the separation easier for some owners. While many people are relieved to be rid of a menacing pet, there are others with strong attachments who find the parting extremely distressing. This holds true, as well, for owners of dogs that must be destroyed. It is painful to know that a dog you loved and cared about has met such a fate.

The following is one family's experience in handling the problem. The story is told by Melanie, a young woman who was an adolescent in the household at the time of the incident:

Our collie, Buffy, was considered high-strung by our veterinarian. We were advised to give him plenty of exercise to allow him to satisfy his herding instincts, but despite our efforts we could not stop his desire to herd cars. As a result, we always walked him on a leash. This frustrated Buffy, who began chewing up shoes, books and other items around the house. After three years his chewing became so intolerable that my mother's solution was to keep him confined to the foyer when no one was home. The dog became increasingly tense and began snapping whenever the phone rang. Whoever answered was likely to be jumped at. Although Buffy looked like he would nip, he never bit anyone.

Then one hot day in August, after Buffy had been in the foyer all day, my mother began to feed him. Just as she put his food down I attempted to swat a fly that was buzzing right behind him. Buffy must have thought he was going to be hit because he whirled around and attacked me, pinning me against the wall. He left a full impression of his teeth in my arm and I was bleeding. Our doctor told us how to clean the bite and advised us that we were required to take the dog to the veterinarian for a ten-day rabies observation.

Buffy did not have rabies but we were worried that he would bite again. The veterinarian told us that once Buffy broke the "taboo" against biting a family member, anyone could be bitten. My sister and I begged to keep the dog anyway, but our parents were adamant about getting rid of him.

We sent Buffy to a sheep ranch in Bogotá, Colombia. The owner, an acquaintance of my father, was happy to have a pedigreed dog to herd his sheep. We got some letters and pictures of Buffy in the beginning. He adjusted well to ranch life, but he continued to bite. The veterinarian there suggested that Buffy may have been going blind, so hand movement near his head startled him. The letters stopped coming after a year, but we were convinced that Buffy had found a good home.

It was a wise decision on this family's part to remove the dog following the first attack. However, had they followed the clues and farmed Buffy out as soon as the first signs of harmful behavior began, they might have saved their daughter a nasty bite.

There are many people, unlike this family, who will not accept the fact that their dog is dangerous; instead, they chalk up each attack to provocation. They are often shocked when someone presses charges and the dog is ordered destroyed or quarantined. The best advice here is to take a realistic view of your pet's behavior. You may save yourself or someone else a great deal of anguish if you act to remove the dog before it can cause serious damage. You will be able to deal with your loss more effectively if you believe you acted responsibly.

When pets must be given away, it is often children who are most affected. They may understand the necessity, but still have a negative emotional response, expressing anger and resentment toward their parents. Younger children may feel that if they misbehave, they too will be ousted from home. Parents should keep in mind that children do not always view loss logically; they may need reassurance that they will not share their pet's fate.

Pet-related bereavement is not caused only by an animal's death. Voluntary and involuntary separation also can lead to grief and sadness; the pet may be alive, but the bonds are broken, nevertheless. When circumstances force one to give up a pet, there may be a great deal of guilt and anger. When the separation is voluntary, it helps to understand that there are times in life when pet ownership is not suitable and that it can be an obstacle to certain goals. Involuntary loss generally is more painful, because there is little to be gained by the separation.

Those who give up their pets voluntarily can help ease their sense of loss by providing the best possible new environment for the animal. Those who have no control over the separation must accept the fact that their pet is no longer with them. In either case, replacement always is a possibility—when the time is right.

9   The Role of the Veterinarian

The relationship between client and veterinarian takes on an added dimension at the time of pet loss. In the ordinary course of practice a veterinarian is responsible for providing medical care for an animal. When a loss has occurred, the practitioner must broaden his scope to be in touch with his client's psychological needs as well. He can represent a sympathetic, knowledgeable figure, possibly the only one in whom a bereaved owner can confide comfortably.

Perhaps the most important psychological service your veterinarian can perform is to provide clearcut, understandable medical explanations that help remove the mystery surrounding your pet's terminal illness or death. Hearing that your cat died of feline infectious peritonitis, for example, may leave you wondering what caused the illness, if surgery could have helped, or whether medication would have altered the outcome. An outline of the facts—that cats cannot survive this common disease which comes on without warning, which is caused by a virus and for which there is no known cure—will provide a more satisfactory explanation. It allows you to deal with the facts and to draw realistic conclusions about the loss, which might otherwise prey on the imagination.

Of course, the facts alone are not enough; the veterinarian must be able to relay the information with a sense of compassion as well. As you learn for the first time that your cat or dog is dying, you may experience a sense of loss as painful as grief following death. A practitioner who delivers the bad news gently, who waits for questions, who takes his time, shows he is sensitive to your feelings. Sometimes just a follow-up telephone call by the veterinarian a day or so after the pet's death will help alleviate the sense of isolation one may feel when struggling with grief reactions that are culturally unacceptable.

When loss occurs, the veterinarian also must be prepared to deal with anger. It may be justified, as in cases of misdiagnosis or maltreatment. But even when there is no question of malpractice, when the proper medical course is strictly followed, the veterinarian can be the target for considerable hostility. Owners should be aware of this tendency to look for a scapegoat, someone to blame for the pet's death, and the veterinarian should understand that he is a natural candidate. Not only is he responsible for medical treatment, but he is the messenger carrying the unpleasant news. Just as the ancient Romans killed the bearers of bad tidings, in modern times we tend to take out our anger on the individuals who tell us what we don't want to hear. By being aware of this human habit, the veterinarian may be able to deal with his anger at having to bear unjustified blame. Understanding this also can allow him to take a calm, measured approach with his clients—the ones in need of support.

As a knowledgeable professional, the veterinarian may help lessen one's unrealistic guilt over the death of a pet. It is common for people to blame themselves, certain that something they did resulted in their animal's illness or death. A veterinarian in Minneapolis spent a great deal of time assuring a couple, newly relocated from Los Angeles, that the primary cause of their pet's death was not pneumonia. They were convinced that the change of climate contributed to the Angora's demise, when, in fact, tests showed that the animal had developed a malignant tumor before they even moved to the northern state.

In issuing explanations, the clinician must forestall unrealistic expectations. If your pet's illness will lead to death, you must be told. You should never be left with the impression that the veterinarian may somehow "magically" cure the animal, when, in fact, there is no hope. You should also expect the practitioner to clarify the financial considerations involved. All possible expenses should be outlined in advance so that you can make realistic decisions about your pet's care.

Sometimes, however, the clearest and kindest of explanations about the animal's condition will be misinterpreted or misunderstood. Overwhelmed by the news that a pet is dead or dying, a distraught owner often asks the same questions over and over—appearing unable to grasp the answers. This is a form of denial, common in the first stages of grief. Failing to hear or understand what the veterinarian is saying allows one to ward off the bad news until it is manageable. An experienced clinician recognizes that this tendency toward denial is a natural defense, and is able to deal with his own frustration at the client's seeming lack of comprehension. He may be able to react with more patience than could be expected of nonprofessionals.

In addition to being sensitive to the owner's general psychological needs, veterinarians can be helpful in other aspects of pet loss. The professional can play an important part with children who have lost a loved pet. He can also help clients manage their shock over sudden death and work through the euthanasia dilemma. In addition, he can arrange for the disposal of a pet's remains and offer advice on pet replacement and non-death-related loss. These various roles are discussed in the following pages, as are the veterinarian's own feelings and fallibilities.

Children and the Family Veterinarian

Children are likely to respond differently from adults to death and dying. A child will have more myths about death, more questions that need to be answered. In some cases parents find it difficult to deal with their children's reactions and turn to the family veterinarian for help. As a figure of authority who has proven in the past that he cared for the family pet, the practitioner is a logical choice; he is someone the child respects and trusts. An emotional parent may not be able to accomplish what this professional can by way of providing explanations and offering reassurances.

As a case in point, a veterinarian in California was called upon for help by the parents of a nine-year-old emotionally disturbed boy, who discovered his dog dead on his property. The youngster thought he was responsible for the dog's death because he underfed the animal. The veterinarian responded to the child's need for reassurance by offering to perform a post-mortem examination. After the autopsy was completed, he was able to tell the troubled youngster that his dog had died from internal injuries, probably as the result of being hit by a car.

Sometimes a veterinarian need only sit down with a child and explain in simple terms what is happening to the pet. In addition to clarifying the facts, this allows the youngster to feel important and worthy of receiving an explanation, and permits him to deal with his loss openly. When children see that death can be discussed freely by someone they respect, they will feel more comfortable doing the same.

When dealing with the sensitive subject of euthanasia, the veterinarian's task is to make clear that neither he nor the child's parents are responsible for the pet's disease or aging. A child can harbor a grudge for years if nobody takes the time to explain the circumstances that prompted the decision for euthanasia.

It is essential to be honest and direct with children in any discussion of pet loss. The veterinarian should provide clear information, without being morbid, about the amount of pain and suffering a pet can expect. Children are capable of understanding a great deal if the explanations are provided in a straightforward manner.

Dealing with Sudden Death

Sudden accidental death accounts for only a small percentage of the average veterinarian's practice, but its impact on owners can be devastating. There is little a veterinarian can do if an animal is struck down on the road or attacked by other animals, except to be, available for the stunned owner. As an active listener, he allows the client to feel that someone cares about his shock and sorrow.

In the wake of an accident, a negligent owner often carries a great deal of guilt. But the veterinarian is trained in medicine, not as a mental-health professional. He can help by being sympathetic and explaining the facts, but he is not in a position to relieve guilt by practicing psychotherapy.

A thoughtful veterinarian will take pains to prepare a client if a suspected routine illness unexpectedly turns out to be terminal. Many will do it in stages, letting the owner know that there is no hope. There are times, however, when a recovering animal takes a sudden turn for the worse or develops a fatal secondary infection. With no preparation, the client often lashes out at the veterinarian, blaming him for the turn of events. Experienced clinicians find that a patient repetition of the facts is the most effective way to help an owner regain his balance and recognize that some things are beyond anyone's control.

There are times when veterinarians must take active roles in helping people over the shock of a pet's unexpected death. Two years ago, a clinician in Ohio received a telephone call from a client requesting emergency treatment for her pet; she had found her kitten unconscious in a drawer, inadvertently shut by a cleaning woman while the family was away for several days. The veterinarian raced over to the house, only to find that the kitten was beyond help—in fact, it had obviously been dead for about twenty-four hours. The client, however, would not accept this diagnosis. So, in order to convince her, the veterinarian injected a shot of adrenalin into the lifeless kitten's heart. When the pet failed to "revive," the woman finally acknowledged that her cat was no longer living. The veterinarian's willingness to make a house call and then to take extra measures went far toward allowing the client to feel that everything possible was done for her pet.

The Veterinarian and Euthanasia

Even when euthanasia seems like the most humane answer, few owners will make the decision to go ahead without professional advice. They rely on the veterinarian to outline the facts about the pet's physical condition, its chance for recovery and future quality of life. While it is not the function of the veterinarian to bring in the final verdict for euthanasia, he certainly can make recommendations based on the facts. However, a reputable clinician will not urge the procedure against the owner's will.

The following interview provides a glimpse into a veterinarian's perspective regarding this issue:

Q: *Can you explain at what point you believe euthanasia should be considered?*

A: If there is no hope for the animal, then I tell the client. If he asks for my recommendations, I weigh all the factors. I consider the psychological health of the owner; what if I get the animal to live for two more weeks? Is that going to pay for the amount of anxiety the owner might have, watching and waiting for the animal to get sick again?

Q: *Do you ever take the initiative in suggesting this measure to the owner?*

A: When I was in veterinary school, a clinic director told us never to be the one to bring up euthanasia first. And from my experience, I know that's the right advice. The owner must feel that he is in control of that decision, that he suggested it first and has the final say.

Q: *Do you ever turn down requests for euthanasia?*

A: I will not perform euthanasia just for the convenience of the owner. When someone calls with that request, my secretary always inquires into the reasons. If the owner is moving or gives some other reason that I do not consider valid, I will not accept the appointment. Nor will I euthanize an animal that I feel I can treat.

Q: *What is your criterion for a "treatable" animal?*

A: Where the disease or disorder can be gotten under control enough so the animal can live out its life in comfort and can still act as a pet.

Q: *What do you tell owners who want to be with their animals as you perform the procedure?*

A: I urge them to stay. This may eliminate nightmares about what it was really like. Some clients are very appreciative. I get thank-you notes for making the whole procedure easier for them. However, I must add that not all clinicians share my views; some prefer to work alone. This matter should be worked out between the client and his veterinarian.

Q: *How about owners who ask you for a way of euthanizing their pets themselves?*

A: Because I make house calls, I will euthanize a pet at home. I definitely do not recommend that owners perform this procedure themselves.

More often than not, the decision to euthanize a pet will take weeks, or even months, with the owner wavering back and forth over this irreversible move. Here, too, the veterinarian must have extreme patience, being prepared for repetitious questions and comments. These discussions serve a function for the owner, providing reinforcement for a very weighty decision. Clients should understand, however, that a veterinarian expects to be paid for extra consultation time, and some may charge for lengthy telephone conversations as well.

Once the course for euthanasia has been set, the owner may enter into a state of anticipatory grieving, showing intense anxiety and agitation. Then, when the time comes for the actual procedure, there is another cycle of distress. As pointed out by Aaron Katcher, M.D., and Marc Rosenberg, V.M.D., in a paper on grief and euthanasia: "The owner's grief is renewed when the animal is brought to the office for the euthanasia procedure or immediately after the animal's death. The clinician must be able to deal with all the manifestations of acute grief, crying, prostration, nervous laughter, numbed incomprehension and accusatory anger. The veterinarian uses the authority of his presence and his sympathetic posture to limit the expression of grief."

In discussions of euthanasia, it is the veterinarian's function to explain the chosen method. Owners should be free to ask questions about the euthanizing agent and expect reassurances that it provides for a quick, painless and, therefore, humane death. At the same time, clients should be encouraged to express their fantasies and fears about euthanasia. Many believe, for example, that the pet knows what is about to happen. It is up to the veterinarian to set the record straight, to explain that animals, unlike humans, do not have an awareness of death. It is the owner's fear, not the animal's, that needs to be confronted.

As a procedural matter, you should expect the veterinarian to request a permission slip giving him the right to perform euthanasia. This prevents any later claim by other family members that the clinician acted without authority.

Following euthanasia, many veterinarians make it a practice to maintain contact with the owner. Many clients still need reassurance that they acted on their pet's behalf, that the animal would not have recovered miraculously. As discussed earlier, euthanasia leads to a great deal of guilt; continued repetition of the facts and a sense of understanding on the part of the veterinarian will go a long way toward lessening that guilt.

If, however, the client shows little sign of recovering after several months, the veterinarian may wish to refer him to a mental health professional for consultation and treatment. While some veterinarians may feel this is overstepping their bounds, Dr. Aaron Katcher, Professor of Psychiatry at the University of Pennsylvania and a consultant to its School of Veterinary Medicine, believes it is within the animal doctor's scope to take such action, providing it is done tactfully. He advised veterinarians to reinforce the fact that the client is not "insane" but needs professional help in dealing with the loss.

Making Arrangements for a Pet's Disposal

Because few owners think of making provisions for their pet's disposal in advance, many are relieved to turn the problem over to the veterinarian following the pet's death. The veterinary practitioner can be of help in several ways. As discussed in Chapter 6, many will make all the provisions for you, from arranging to pick up the deceased animal at your home to providing for disposal at a pet cemetery or crematorium. Some will hold your animal under refrigeration until you are ready to decide on the method of disposal. If you know you want to bury your pet in your backyard, the veterinarian can keep your pet's remains, if necessary, until the ground thaws. The practitioner will often charge a small fee for this service, but most pet owners find it worth the expense, reporting that relying on a professional at this time saves them a great deal of distress.

Helping in Replacing, Locating and Adopting Pets

As an expert in animal care, the veterinarian is a natural source of help with pet replacement. He can issue advice on breeds that would be most suitable for your family and where to find the best of them. He can give you pointers on caring for the new animal, for even the most experienced pet owners may forget what goes into raising a puppy or kitten. And replacing a pet with an unfamiliar breed may be like starting over.

As a precautionary step, the veterinary physician can examine any animal you are considering adopting to make sure it is healthy. (It is advisable to take this step before making a commitment, even if you are well acquainted with the former owners.)

If you are searching for a missing animal, the veterinarian is an excellent source of help. In the course of a day, the practitioner and his staff may see twenty or thirty animals; it is entirely possible that a missing pet may turn up in another client's possession. Or, if you want to adopt a pet or put one out for adoption, the veterinarian's office can serve as a clearinghouse. Sometimes, clinicians find unwanted animals on their doorsteps that may be perfectly healthy animals and suitable for adoption.

Dr. Jack Anteleyes, a small-animal practitioner who runs an animal hospital in an urban setting, reports that at least once a week people abandon animals on his premises. Some simply open the door to the clinic, push their animals into the waiting room and disappear into waiting cars. Others throw their animals over the fence of an adjacent exercise run, to be found by the clinic staff the following morning. The abandoned animals are examined, treated, if necessary, and held at the clinic. The staff keeps an up-to-date file of people who are interested in adopting pets or whose animals have died or disappeared. When the animal is ready for adoption, a staff member contacts prospective owners until a suitable home is found. In the last twenty years, this thoughtful service has resulted in approximately six hundred adoptions.

Even if the veterinarian cannot provide "instant" adoptive pets, many have bulletin boards or notebooks displaying lost-and-found notices, pictures of animals up for adoption and other pertinent information to match pets with owners. When a veterinarian arranges an adoption, he can frequently provide the new owner with data on the pet's medical history, behavioral problems or eccentricities. Knowing in advance what to expect from an adopted pet can make the adjustment a great deal easier.

A veterinarian instrumental in arranging a successful adoption can derive a considerable amount of satisfaction, as in the following story:

Popi, a wirehaired terrier, escaped from his owner's yard by digging a hole under a metal mesh fence and wriggling through the opening. He had managed this trick only once before, returning a few hours later. This time, however, after twenty-four hours' absence, the Wilkes family was seriously worried that they would never see the animal again.

They conducted a thorough search through newspaper advertisements, neighborhood posters and their veterinarian's office, with no success. After two months, the family reluctantly decided to get another dog, with the stipulation that it be the same breed. Mrs. Wilkes phoned her veterinarian, Dr. Martin, to ask him to be on the lookout for a good-dispositioned wirehaired terrier.

The veterinarian was a good choice; he donated several hours each week helping out at the local animal shelter. A week later, Dr. Martin phoned. The shelter had obtained two wirehaired terriers from the pound that week. He wanted Mrs. Wilkes to see them, although he doubted that either would be suitable. He hadn't examined the dogs, but had been told that one was rather old and lethargic, and the other extremely high-strung, and possibly suffering from malnutrition. Mrs. Wilkes went to the shelter the following day with very little hope that she would return home with a new pet. The shelter's director confirmed her pessimism. The older terrier was ill and no longer up for adoption. The other was nasty and snappish and not likely to be suitable for a family.

She decided to look at him anyway, so the handler brought him out, barking and yapping. When Mrs. Wilkes saw the dog, her heart lurched. And suddenly, the terrier began to whimper and strain at his leash. There was no doubt that owner and pet knew each other, despite the long months apart and the change in Popi's appearance. Mrs. Wilkes further identified her pet by a small cyst on his chest.

While she was still at the shelter, she called Dr. Martin to tell him the amazing news and to determine whether Popi's personality had been permanently damaged by any maltreatment or malnutrition he had suffered. The veterinarian suggested that she bring him over immediately for an examination. After making a thorough evaluation, Dr. Martin assured his client that with good food, attention and time, Popi would be his old self. The rest of the Wilkes family had a remarkable surprise waiting for them that night.

The Veterinarian's Feelings

A veterinarian with an active practice will see approximately two or three cases of pet loss each week, brought about either by natural causes or euthanasia. He may appear to be unemotional and highly professional when confronted with an animal patient's death. But a veterinarian is subject to the same feelings and emotions as the rest of the population, and can be as disturbed as the owner at the death of a cat or dog he has treated since birth, for example. Many clinicians have had their own personal pet-loss experiences and are well aware of the resulting stress. The task of performing euthanasia can be particularly upsetting. The following excerpt from an interview with a veterinarian provides insight into her feelings on this matter:

Q: *What role do you see yourself playing immediately before and after euthanizing an animal?*
A: I see myself being incredibly professional and thorough. That is my job.

Q: *How about the psychological aspects? Obviously you must get involved on some level as we all do, no matter how professional we are.*
A: I really hate doing it. I hate feeling like I have the power to do that. Sometimes I will build anxieties a day or so in advance, and afterwards, although I am very professional, I am extremely apologetic. In fact, when I first began to practice, I wanted to cry with my clients. But now I just go home and feel rotten for the rest of the night.

Of course, every veterinarian reacts according to his emotional makeup and some are able to view an animal's death as part of the hazards of the profession. What really matters is that the veterinarian understands what his own feelings are about death so as to help the owner cope with his. As Katcher and Rosenberg point out in discussing euthanasia: "However the procedure is performed, the actions and words of the veterinarian will leave a greater impression on the owner than all the skillful, dedicated treatment of his pet."

Can the Veterinarian Always Be Trusted?

Veterinarians make mistakes just as other people do. Unfortunately, an error by a medical professional can result in loss of life or permanent physical damage. While many owners become angry over pet loss, unjustifiably seeking someone to blame, there are certainly times when a client's accusations of malpractice are warranted.

If you suspect that your veterinarian was responsible for mistreating your pet, there are several things you can do:

1. Tell your veterinarian your suspicions, but hold the discussions in person. Telephone communications under these circumstances generally are unsatisfactory. Proceed calmly; you will accomplish more with civil communication than with high-strung accusations.

2. If you remain dissatisfied, discuss the matter with the veterinarian's superior, if there is one.

3. As a further step, you can report your complaint to the grievance committee or your state Veterinary Medical Association, or your city or county veterinary professional organization.

4. For stronger action, you can notify your State Board of Veterinary Examiners. This agency has the power to suspend or revoke a veterinarian's license if such action is warranted.

5. You can consult with a lawyer about your chances for recovering monetary damages, for both the fair market value of the animal and emotional distress. But you should be certain of your facts. A lawsuit takes time and money, and current case law suggests that the chances are not good for recovery beyond what an animal such as yours would bring on the market. If you do plan to consult a lawyer, act immediately before disposal of the pet's body. The lawyer may advise you to take the remains to a second veterinarian for an autopsy, or he may want you to gather or preserve other evidence of possible malpractice.

6. Finally, look around for another veterinarian, unless the first one can prove to your complete satisfaction that your accusations are unwarranted. You should have full confidence in your veterinarian's professional conduct.

A positive rapport between a veterinarian and his client is crucial in pet loss or impending loss situations. The veterinarian must deal not only with the physical and medical needs of the pet, but with the emotional needs of the owner as well.

Sometimes, owners just need their veterinarians to be good listeners. Following a pet's death, many search for a sympathetic ear. Friends or relatives may grow impatient, but a veterinarian, by nature of his profession and experience, is likely to offer the much-needed understanding. This contact allows the owner to deal openly with his feelings in a tolerant, sympathetic environment.

Medical explanations in lay terms will help the owner understand the pet's condition and a sympathetic approach will allow him to feel comfortable expressing his distress and anxiety.

Emphasizing the fact that animals have shorter life spans than humans, that they live more perilous lives and that some illnesses cannot be controlled will help the owner accept the loss and put it into perspective. That is a crucial step in resolving grief.

Epilogue

The following article by the late Eleanor Perry appeared in the Living Section of *The New York Times* on June 28, 1978. We believe it is a most fitting ending to this book:

Hail and Farewell: An Epitaph for Lulu

The risk, of course, is to appear sentimental. But why? Because she was a dog? "Only a dog," as some people say. Does one measure out feelings according to species?

There are other phones in the apartment but whenever I went to one of them you dragged yourself up onto your feet, one hind leg paralyzed, the other almost, and hobbled after me. By the time I had dialed you were there. I couldn't close the door. I had never closed a door on you in your life. In the end we went back to my workroom, where you always began the mornings lying on the rug behind my typewriter. I arranged your death on the desk phone in a voice I might have used for arranging to have the laundry picked up.

"I want to be with her when you give her the injection," I told the doctor.

We'd had this discussion before, a few months ago when you were in his clinic for surgery and my terror was that you'd die there without me.

"I won't break down," I promised him again. "I'll be very calm. She won't pick up any vibrations from me."

The doctor said we could bring you in that afternoon and

then he gave me the telephone number of the crematory which would take care of "the body." My stomach knotted. I had not yet thought of you as "the body."

The voice at the crematory was kindly and efficient. "Would you like the ashes returned to you?"

I had not thought of you as "the ashes" either. "No," I said.

"Then we'll bury them here in our garden. Would you like a marker?"

"No."

There was one more call to make. We had often been rejected by taxi drivers when you were young and beautiful and impeccably groomed. What would the drivers say now when they saw your poor misshapen body with great patches of hide peeling off it and the open sores? I hired a car to take us to the clinic.

So only a few days after your birthday (Ann had sent you twelve tulips, "for twelve happy years") you were going to be put to death and I had arranged it. It was my right as your owner. Owner and owned? In my head those words had never before applied to us. We were devoted companions. Because of you I knew every glade and hollow in Central Park. Because of me you explored the passageways of Venice and the stony shores of Cap Ferrat.

You were typecast in a film I wrote and played yourself, a standard poodle with a tail like a black chrysanthemum. Like any leading lady you got your key-light and your close-ups. We adjusted to each other's moods. You pranced ahead of me mischievous and full of joy when I was happy, withdrew in dignified silence when I wasn't. I played when you brought me your ball and kept an eye out for the police when you wanted to run free without a leash. We had our routines: my Scotch, your milk before sleeping, breakfast toast together on my bed.

A few months ago the morning came when you couldn't

leap up onto the bed. I saw you fall back to the floor and your look of astonished humiliation. After that I lifted you up and lifted you down again. Then the day came when you wouldn't walk farther than the entrance to the park and, later, the day when stepping off the curb was too precarious for you.

I tried to pretend nothing was changing. We played ball in the apartment but one night, limping and falling, you gave up and refused to retrieve it. So there was no more ball-playing and in a little while no more bones—not after we found your mouth bloody and two of your teeth on the rug. Your bark disappeared—that mighty deafening fuss you'd always make to greet a guest or a package. Now when the doorbell rang there was only a hoarse little rumble in your throat.

It was all right. With the help of drugs and painkillers we could live with all of that. It was the blood we couldn't live with. Organs ruptured and blood poured out of you, a worse hemorrhage each time. Alarming lumps and swellings appeared all over your body. Old age beat us out, Lulu. Inevitability beat us. Death-is-a-part-of-life beat us.

The three who loved you best, Mickey and Ann and I, drove uptown with you on that spring afternoon. In a season when so many things are beginning to live, I had arranged for you to die. Would any season have been the right one? Not the winter when your romping black body was breathtaking against the snow, not the summer when you raced along the beach barking at the waves, not the autumn when perfectly on point you stalked squirrels in the woods.

Mickey had brought along your big blue towel—the one she used when she bathed you and spread on the terrace for you to lie on when the tiles were cold. She carried you and the towel into the clinic and into the examining room and put you down gently on the stainless steel table. When the doctor who had known you all your life came in you wagged your gray rope of a tail, all the proud petals gone.

"Do you mind if I don't do it?" the doctor asked me. He pressed his lips to your topknot. "Take care, Lulu," he whispered. The other doctor, his young colleague, came in to give you a shot to make you sleepy. Mickey could not bear to watch. She reminded us to wrap you in your towel "afterwards," embraced you fiercely and went into the waiting room to weep. Ann and I stayed, holding you, talking to you.

You didn't get sleepy. Your once lustrous black eyes, now milky with cataracts, rolled about towards our voices. Your breath came in hard rapid pants and your pink tongue, the only thing about you unchanged, licked our hands and faces.

"She's a very large dog," the young doctor said. "She's fighting it." *Fighting it?* My God, then she knows! She doesn't want to die! Stop everything right now, I wanted to shout, we're taking her home! I didn't shout. I heard myself lying to you instead. "Everything's going to be all right, Lulu, everything's going to be just fine." I was relieved when the doctor gave you another shot. I wanted it to be over. I wanted to stop pretending I was not the killer I was.

Soon after that your breathing slowed and your head drooped. We held on to you while the doctor shaved a few inches of fur off your foreleg and inserted a needle into your vein. I had never seen death before. It doesn't come or arrive. One instant it is not there, the next instant it is there. The true freeze-frame. The doctor covered you with the blue towel.

Goodbye, sweet girl.

Later, Mickey and Ann and I said all the words: "It had to be done." "She had a wonderful life." "We all gave her such a good life."

But I was the one who gave you death, Lulu. Is there such a thing as a good death?

Appendix A: Frequently Asked Questions and Answers

The following are questions commonly asked by pet lovers. For convenience they are grouped by subject matter according to the chapters in this book.

Attachment

Q: *Do people become attached as strongly to birds, hamsters and other pets as they do to cats and dogs? Do they feel their loss as much?*

A: Attachments may be made to any pet—parrot, hamster, gerbil, rabbit, tropical fish, to name some common ones—as long as the person receives emotional gratification from the pet. However, it should be noted that pets that respond to their owners usually generate a greater feeling of attachment because they can give as well as receive affection. By the same token, the loss of any pet can stir up grief reactions, but the degree of distress is usually linked to the strength of the tie.

Q: *Our son was brokenhearted when our neighbor's dog was killed by a car. Tommy used to play with her and walk her sometimes after school. Is his reaction unusual, considering it was not our dog?*

A: Your son's feelings are not at all unusual. The nature of attachment between children and pets—affection, unconditional acceptance and loyalty—lends itself to the formation of a strong emotional tie. This can be true even when the animal belongs to someone else, if there was a great deal of contact and affection between the two. The grief reaction in your son's case should be dealt with as seriously as if he were the dog's owner.

Q: *Is it possible to form a strong attachment to a pet without being aware of it? I never paid much attention to our cat but after we lost her to leukemia I felt very bad. Why am I having such a late reaction?*

A: People tend to take their pets for granted, possibly because animals have undemanding natures and can be acquired with relative ease. You probably cared for your cat, you just never thought about your feelings very much. It seems to be human nature that we accept what we have and value what we have lost.

Q: *I never had a special attachment to my miniature schnauzer, Poppy, until my last child left home. Now I take her everywhere, buy her special toys, sleep with her and worry excessively about her health. My husband says I care more about her welfare than I do his. Is this, as he says, an unhealthy relationship?*

A: Whether an attachment to a pet is healthy or unhealthy depends upon a number of variables. How much are you allowing Poppy to interfere with your life? Has she affected your relationship with your husband or other close friends or relatives? Do you turn down invitations if Poppy is not included? Does she occupy your thoughts over most other matters? Frequently pets may be used as substitutes for absent family members to counter the loneliness brought on by the separation. There is nothing unhealthy about that unless the relationship interferes with daily functioning. If you believe that is what's happening, you might want to discuss the situation with a therapist.

Q: *What can I say to people who do not take my feelings seriously and laugh when I talk about missing my cat, Otis, who died six months ago?*

A: There are some people who cannot appreciate the human-pet relationship. There are also those who have difficulty in dealing with losses and separation. They may be unable to comprehend the grief and sadness that you are experiencing because they are uncomfortable with their own grief reactions. There is really nothing that you need to say to others to justify your feelings. By continuing the discussion, you are reinforcing the other person's negative behavior and encouraging obvious insensitivity.

Q: *My sister has diabetes and she is sure that her cat has the disease as well. She keeps seeing signs that I don't think are there. Is she overreacting?*

A: Assuming that the cat has been examined and found to be healthy, your sister's reaction is, indeed, an exaggeration. Some people project their own feelings, fears and worries on animals to whom they are greatly attached. In many instances this merely represents concern for the welfare of a helpless dependent. However, in some cases of exaggerated attachment, the pet "is" the person; and whatever affects one affects the other, because in the owner's view they are one and the same. Such intense projection is often the symptom of a deeply rooted psychological problem that may require professional help.

Separation

Q: *I am embarrassed asking this, but is it possible to feel worse about a pet's death than the death of a relative?*

A: There is no need to feel embarrassed, as we all react to different losses in different ways. A pet that has provided warmth, love and emotional security may evoke a stronger grief reaction upon its death than a relative with whom one has had little emotional or physical contact. While the loss of a pet is not equated with that of a human, the nature of the grief reaction may be very similar.

Q: *My cat, Snowball, seems to be depressed and listless ever since our Labrador, Blackfoot, died. Is this possible, or am I imagining this reaction?*

A: According to Dr. Peter Borchelt, an animal behaviorist, separation behavior may indeed show up in pets. The surviving animal tends to mope, pick at food and even search for its lost companion. The pet may even mimic the lost animal's actions. This pattern of behavior resembles human grief reaction; when it occurs the lonely pet needs a great deal of attention and affection. If the behavior persists, it would be wise to consult a veterinarian or an animal behaviorist.

Q: *How long should I expect to feel unhappy over my dog's death?*

A: The amount of time it takes to get over a pet's death varies considerably. Some people can deal quickly with the loss, while others require a year or more to resolve their grief. Obviously it has a great deal to do with the degree of attachment, the way the loss is treated and the emotional makeup of the individual. As a rule, though (and remember, all rules have exceptions), most people are ready to move ahead within ten months of pet loss.

Children and Pet Loss

Q: *How can we prepare our children for the fact that our dog is terminally ill?*

A: The general rule to follow in explaining illness or death to children is to do so honestly and in terms they can understand. Your youngsters may even be helped by speaking directly to the veterinarian in charge of the pet's treatment. Encourage them to ask questions. This will help take the mystery out of what is happening, since children's fantasies are often worse than reality. A conference with your veterinarian also will give your children the opportunity to learn how to share their feelings openly.

Q: *We are thinking of starting a family. Our Malamute, Alex, has always been well-behaved but we are worried that he might be jealous of the new baby. Are we being too fearful, or is there a chance that the infant will be in danger?*

A: This is frequently asked by parents-to-be. According to Dr. Peter Borchelt, the probability of a well-trained pet harming an infant is rather small. There are, however, certain behavioral indicators in pets that might predict potential problems. An animal that is frightened by sudden movements might be threatened by the young child's impulsive activities. Some dogs are extremely sensitive to pain and skin pressure; those that snap when being brushed or groomed may do so when handled roughly by a child. The pet that is overly protective of one of the spouses might react to competition from the child by turning threatening or vicious. As a rule, infants do not evoke as much negative behavior in animals as older children do, with their curious and exploring ways. But no matter what the pet's personality is like, children should be taught to approach with care. There is no way to guarantee the reaction of a pet that is mishandled.

Q: *Is it true that children's reactions to pet loss help them with losses later in life?*

A: There is strong evidence, based on data from many grief therapists, that pet loss provides a role model—something like a dress rehearsal—for children to deal with subsequent losses. The death of a pet is usually a person's first experience with loss. Getting through the episode successfully will indicate to a child that other losses—painful though they may be—can also be survived.

Q: *After a pet dies, what questions are children most likely to ask?*

A: With their normal curiosity, children often wonder where the pet is, what it is thinking, if the animal is safe, if they were responsible for the death, and, most common of all, if they will ever see the pet again. These questions must be answered honestly and directly on the level of the child's understanding. Most children can sense a lie or when issues are being avoided.

Q: *Should children be permitted to observe their parents' expression of grief or should the distress be minimized?*

A: Children should understand that their parents have feelings too. This will help them recognize that grief is a natural response to loss at any age.

Q: *My daughter, Shari, buried her pet hamster in the park over a year ago. She still avoids the spot. Isn't it taking her a long time to get over the loss?*

A: The answer to this question depends upon your daughter's age and prior experiences with death. Usually, pre-adolescent children want to visit pets' burial sites. Shari's reluctance is suggestive of some fear. Perhaps there are unanswered questions in her mind about death and burial which you need to explore with her.

Q: *As a teacher, I would like to know how to handle the situation when a youngster comes to class and tells us that a pet has died.*

A: The teacher—who is seen as an authority figure with all the answers—has great impact on children's emotional growth. When a child loses a pet and chooses to talk about it in school, the teacher may want to hold a group discussion about the incident. This will allow the other children to share similar experiences and provide reassurance for the saddened youngster that he is not alone. The child will also learn that it is acceptable to talk about the loss and not be embarrassed or ashamed.

Q: *Just after our dog died, our son started having difficulty in school. My husband thinks Tommy is just looking for attention, but isn't it likely that he is reacting to the loss?*

A: Distress over pet loss may very well show up in declining performance and behavior problems in school. The loss may cause depression and anxiety which lead to shortened attention span and restlessness. Children may not even be aware of what is causing the problem, but a perceptive parent or teacher will quickly make the association with pet loss. The child should be encouraged to talk about what is troubling him. If school problems persist for more than a few weeks, the youngster should be seen by a mental health professional.

Handling Imminent or Sudden Death

Q: *What instructions should I give my children in case they are home alone and our pet has an accident?*

A: Children should be instructed to use the telephone, just as they would for any emergency. The telephone numbers of the veterinarian, a neighbor or nearby relative should be conspicuously posted nearby. Children should be advised that the first step in trying to help an injured or dying pet is to call for help and obtain assistance.

Q: *Is there any way of preparing in advance for the sudden loss of a pet?*

A: There is really no way of anticipating sudden death. You cannot have it on your mind constantly that your cat or dog will meet with an accident or develop a sudden illness. The best preparation is to gain an understanding of the grieving process, so when the time comes you will know how to deal with your feelings.

Q: *My wife and I took our first vacation in years and left our children and dog in the care of a woman who has babysat for us many times before. Even though we were three thousand miles away from home, my wife still feels guilty because Mopsy, our dachshund, ran outside and was struck and killed by a truck. What can I tell my wife to make her realize that she was not at fault?*

A: This is an extremely common situation. Presumably your wife left instructions for the babysitter, so in reality she is not to blame for the accident. However, although our minds tell us one thing, our feelings often give us entirely different signals. Your wife is, no doubt, blaming herself for "abandoning" the family, for taking pleasure for herself at the expense of a helpless animal. She may also be assuming guilt brought on by a subconscious fear that it could have been one of the children who ran out and suffered the same fate. Once she recognizes that she did not "betray" her family, that she was entitled to a vacation, and that she must turn her anger away from herself, she will probably be able to put the episode in perspective.

Euthanasia

Q: *We are having a terrible disagreement in our family about euthanasia. When it comes right down to it, isn't euthanasia the same as murdering a defenseless pet?*

A: In its most literal sense, euthanasia is the taking of life, and, as such, some people compare it with "murder." As many others see it, though, euthanasia is a method of humanely ending a pet's life because of serious irreversible illness, chronic pain or other situation in which the animal's quality of life is being significantly decreased. Most veterinarians are trained to provide as peaceful, painless and humane death as possible, thus giving a dignified end to a pet that might instead be suffering.

Q: *Should I stay with my pet as it is being euthanized?*

A: Although some veterinarians are concerned about their clients' reactions, if you feel that you are emotionally prepared and willing to witness the procedure, then by all means do so. It can be a very comforting experience for you and your pet. If, however, you do not want to be present, it is perfectly acceptable to leave the procedure to the veterinarian. The decision does not indicate the degree of feeling for your animal, but rather your own personal preference. It should be pointed out, though, that being present, or at least seeing the pet afterward, provides closure and reality to the circumstance. There is no chance to imagine that by some miracle your pet is alive and well. Facing the fact of death always helps in resolving grief.

Q: *What if I want to be with my pet during euthanasia but my veterinarian discourages me?*

A: Make every effort to explain your reasons for wanting to attend your pet. If the veterinarian continues to oppose your attendance, find out why. If you are not persuaded by his reasons, consider consulting with another practitioner. Most professionals will cooperate with a client's wishes in this matter.

Putting a Pet to Rest

Q: *I want to bury my cat in a pet cemetery, but my friends think I'm sentimental and extravagant. Are my plans so unusual?*

A: There is nothing odd about cemetery burial for a pet; it is done everyday in over five hundred cemeteries throughout the country. If you can afford the expense and it gives you satisfaction, you need not defend or justify your actions. Your cat obviously means a great deal to you. Arranging for its permanent resting place is an investment in your own sense of well-being. Your friends, no doubt, invest in certain "nonessentials" that add to the quality of their lives, so why can't you?

Q: *I heard somewhere that it is illegal to bury a pet in a backyard. Is that a federal, state or local law?*

A: Generally, it is the individual municipality or local health board that establishes laws to govern backyard burial. Your local government or police department will have the information. Before going ahead, you might want to consult an undertaking establishment for tips on proceeding properly. For example, if a grave is too shallow, it might be uncovered by children or animals, causing a serious health hazard.

Q: *My dog, Romney, is still alive, but I would like to make arrangements in advance for us to be buried side-by-side. Is this possible?*

A: There is at least one cemetery in the country, Bonheur Memorial Park in Elkridge, Maryland, that provides for this type of burial. Since its opening in 1935, some eight thousand pets and fifteen owners have been buried there, and the proprietors report that one hundred more pet owners have made reservations. Human remains are handled by a licensed funeral home and brought to the burial grounds. You may wish to write to Bonheur, or to the International Association of Pet Cemeteries, (27 W 150 North Avenue, West Chicago, Illinois 60185) for information on other cemeteries that may provide this service.

Q: *After all my dog and I have been through, I can't simply discard him. I want to make some gesture for his disposal but I have no backyard, and, besides, I don't*

*have the strength to dig a grave. Also my budget is
rather limited, so burial in a pet cemetery is out. What
are my options?*

A: Why not arrange to have your pet cremated and the remains scattered in a pet cemetery? The cost is around
$30 (at this time) and you can visit the cemetery when-
ever you wish. For a small additional fee, you might
want your pet's cremated remains placed in an urn and
returned to you. Many people are very satisfied with this
method of disposal.

Replacement

Q: *Can a new pet really take the place of one that died or
disappeared?*

A: A new pet can never replace one that is gone. But a new
animal can introduce a new relationship and a new set of
feelings. Many people think that replacing a pet will immediately soften and erase the grief reaction. This is not
true; people still grieve and go through various types of
mourning reactions even if there is a new pet at home.

Q: *How long should we wait before getting another dog?
Our West Highland terrier died a month ago.*

A: The best time to get a new pet is when you feel you are
ready. Although this may sound vague, if you get a pet
too soon, or half-heartedly, you may be doing yourself
and the animal a disservice. How do you know if you are
ready? Once you work out your grief feelings and start
thinking about a new animal in your life, you have be-
gun to prepare for another commitment.

Q: *Is it wrong to replace a pet with the same breed?*

A: Not at all. In fact, it is quite commonly done. Owners are
familiar with the breed and prefer an animal with the
same tendencies. On the other hand, some people report

that they are bothered by memories cropping up over and over again. If you think you can treat the same breed of dog as a separate being from your former pet, there is nothing wrong with choosing this type of replacement.

Q: *My family wants to get another dog to replace the retriever that we had for eleven years, but I think we will be forgetting Mocha. Don't I have a legitimate complaint?*

A: Many people believe that a new pet will erase the memory of the old. This is just not true. Introducing a new pet into the family simply means that a new relationship is going to be formed; the old relationship will still be remembered and valued.

Q: *Our dog, Boozer, is getting older. Should we get a new dog in preparation for Boozer's death?*

A: This is debatable. Many people are able to introduce a new pet into the household without incident. Frequently, however, the newcomer will have to compete very strongly for its territory. The older animal may feel threatened, even to the point of suffering, by the new arrival and the intrusion into its life. Many people feel that a second pet will soften the blow of the loss when it occurs. This is not necessarily true; the grief reactions may be just as intense. Therefore, it may be more advisable to deal with your feelings when your pet dies, think carefully about introducing a new animal into your home, and then make the choice.

Q: *Having just lost a cat, I want another, but I dread going through an episode of illness and loss again. Will my feelings change?*

A: There is always the risk of losing something that we love; that is the price of commitment. But there is much more to be lost by not establishing other relationships, by protecting ourselves from all pain. Grief and sadness are normal reactions to loss, but those feelings usually resolve themselves in time. Perhaps when you have put some distance between yourself and your loss reactions, you will feel more comfortable getting another animal.

Q: *A business colleague just learned that her ten-year-old dachshund has only a few months to live, and naturally she is very upset. Some of us thought of taking up a collection and surprising her with another dog after she loses Frankie. Is this advisable?*

A: It is a nice thought but you might be overstepping your bounds. Your friend may be unprepared to take on another dependent animal after undergoing the strain and worry associated with a terminally ill pet. Don't abandon the idea, but explore it with her instead of making it a surprise.

Loss Unrelated to Death

Q: *We found a kitten this summer. Will it be hard on our children if we give it away, rather than take it back to the city with us?*

A: If it is impossible to take the pet with you, make preparations well in advance for adopting it out. Explain to the children exactly what is being done and why, and give them a chance to question your motives. In addition, allow them to explore and respond to the feelings they have, which may range from extreme anger to depression. On the other hand, children are more resilient than we may think, and they usually recover from these episodes more quickly and with better results than adults.

Q: *We had a terrible snowstorm last month and I was home alone with a bad cold. Fluffy, our cocker spaniel,*

*scratched to go out, so I just opened the door and let
her go because I was too sick to walk her. She must have
lost her scent because she never came back. Will I ever
get over these terrible guilt feelings?*

A: Rest assured that guilt tends to resolve itself with the passage of time. However, there are ways in which you can hasten the resolution. First, recognize that you didn't lose your dog intentionally; there were justifiable circumstances—your health—that prompted you to act as you did. Next, do all that you can to try and recover Fluffy. Finally, turn the episode into a learning experience so it won't be duplicated in the future. If your guilt feelings persist with great intensity for more than a few months, it would be advisable to seek help.

About the Veterinarian

Q: *I would like to discuss my feelings about pet loss with
my veterinarian. Is this taking up too much of his time?*

A: Veterinarians are prepared to be available to pet owners and their families under many circumstances. A practitioner's job is not limited to animal medical treatment only; the professional's job is to educate owners and to be on hand when problems arise. Your veterinarian might not be able to speak with you immediately upon request, but he will probably make time shortly afterward. If, after your meeting, your veterinarian thinks you have problems beyond his scope, he may recommend that you seek help from a trained psychotherapist.

Q: *Do you think veterinarians experience difficulties over
the death of an animal in their care, or are they somewhat hardened to these situations?*

A: Many veterinarians have chosen their field of medicine because of their sensitivity and feelings about animals. They can experience distress, just as owners do, over an animal's injury, loss or death. As caregivers, clinicians may not want to show their feelings, fearing to appear weak and undermine their clients' confidence. However, many report intense stress, particularly when performing euthanasia.

Q: *When I found out that my cat's condition was hopeless, I expected my veterinarian to decide for euthanasia. But he said the decision was up to me. Doesn't he know better than I what should happen to my cat?*

A: The function of the veterinarian is not to determine your cat's fate, but to provide enough information to allow you to make an intelligent decision. Supposing your veterinarian insisted that euthanasia was the only course, but you were opposed to it. How would you feel then?

Miscellaneous

Q: *If people have had pets for centuries, why is it that pet-loss difficulties are just being recognized and studied?*

A: There are two reasons that come to mind to account for this: First, the subject of death and dying—once very much avoided—is now being examined openly. Within the last few decades, the management of death has evoked an outpouring of interest and research in literature, education, medicine and the social-science fields. Second, mental health professionals are beginning to recognize how meaningful, both physically and psychologically, pets can be to human beings and how complicated and longlasting separation reactions can be. With investigation underway in both fields, it is natural to link the two and to study human reaction to pet loss.

Q: *What can I do to insure that my pet will be cared for if I die first?*

A: There are several possibilities to consider. You can arrange with a friend or relative to assume responsibility for your cat or dog. To assure that this will work out, you should make certain advance arrangements beyond merely mentioning it in your will. Make sure the person agrees to the idea, and if possible leave an outright bequest that will cover food, housing and veterinary care for the life expectancy of the animal. Those who do not have a friend or relative willing to assume this responsibility often request in their will that their animals be humanely euthanized immediately upon their death. This request should be made also in a letter to the veterinarian and a friend willing to assist with this step. These arrangements should be spelled out in advance because many veterinarians are unwilling to perform euthanasia on a healthy animal. Another possibility is to leave a bequest in your will to cover expenses for your pet at a retirement home. In this type of facility—usually a converted house—the pet can live out the rest of its life uncaged in the companionship of other animals, looked after by a caretaker. Information about these facilities can be obtained from your veterinarian or local animal shelter. If you wish further information about post-mortem arrangements for taking care of your pet, you can request a reprint of the article "Arrangements for Pets in Your Will" by Murdaugh Stuart Madden that appeared in the *Humane Society News* in Fall, 1978 (write to: Office of the General Counsel, Humane Society of the United States, 2100 L Street N.W., Washington, D.C. 20037).

Q: *What can I do to commemorate my pet? I recognize that this is not a human loss, but I had great affection for my cat and I would like to make some small gesture to remember him.*

A: More and more people are memorializing their pets, recognizing that this satisfies a need to keep good memories alive. The following are some suggestions:

—Plant a small tree or shrub in your yard or local countryside. You might even want to affix a plaque with the pet's name, dates of birth and death, and a simple message.

—Donate funds for equipment to an animal hospital, shelter or other pet-related facility.

—Donate funds for medical research in the disease that claimed your pet's life.

—Arrange to have a painting or sketch of your pet copied from a photograph; or arrange for handiwork such as needlepoint to be designed in your pet's likeness.

—Some people commemorate the anniversary of their pet's death according to their religious traditions or in other less formal ways such as a visit to a burial site.

Q: *I am not a pet owner but have several pet-loving friends. I would like to do "the right thing" when one of my friends loses a pet. Does one mimic a human loss—send a card, flowers or possibly a contribution to an animal shelter?*

A: This is a question that many people wonder about. Your response would depend upon your friends' loss reaction. As you know, some people tolerate pet loss quite well, others are deeply distressed. If you feel that an expression of sympathy will show a bereaved friend that you understand his sense of loss, then it is entirely appropriate. The extent of your condolences will depend upon your relationship with the owner; it can range from a telephone call or note, to a visit, to a contribution to a pet-related organization. It is your show of interest that matters.

References

Beadle, Muriel. *The Cat: A Complete Authoritative Compendium of Information about Domestic Cats.* New York: Simon & Schuster, 1977.

Bowlby, John. *Attachment and Loss,* volume III:Loss. New York: Basic Books, 1980.

Canadian Veterinary Medical Association. "The Euthanasia of Dogs and Cats: A Statement by the Humane Practices Committee of the Canadian Veterinary Medical Association." *Canad. Vet. J.,* vol. 19 (1978), pp. 164–68.

Carr, Arthur, et al., eds. *Anticipatory Grief.* New York: Columbia University Press, 1974.

——— , et al., eds. *Bereavement—Its Psychosocial Aspects.* New York: Columbia University Press, 1975.

Corso v. Crawford Dog and Cat Hospital, 415 New York Suppl 2nd 182. 1979.

Fiorone, Fiorenzo. *The Encyclopedia of Dogs.* New York: Lippincott and Crowell, 1970.

Fischer, Arlene. "When a Pet's Death Hurts Its Master." *The New York Times,* May 8, 1980.

——— . "Mourning the Loss of a Pet." *Pure-Bred Dogs American Kennel Gazette,* vol. 97, no. 10 (1980), pp. 57–8.

Fox, Michael W. "Understanding Your Pet—Making Your Most Difficult Decision." *McCall's,* Jan. 1981.

Friedman, Erika, et al. "Animal Companions and One-Year Survival of Patients after Discharge From a Coronary-Care Unit." *Public Health Reports,* vol. 95, no. 4 (1980), pp. 307–12.

Frost & Sullivan, Inc. *Pet Care Products and Services Market Report,* Dec. 1980.

Grollman, Earl. *Explaining Death to Children.* Boston: Beacon Press, 1967.

Gunby, P. "Pets for Cardiac Therapeutics." *J.A.M.A.,* vol. 241 (1979), p. 438.

Katcher, Aaron, and Marc A. Rosenberg. "Euthanasia and the Management of the Client's Grief." *Compendium on Continuing Education,* vol. 1, no. 12 (1979), pp. 887–90.

Keane, John. *Sherlock Bones.* Philadelphia and New York: J.B. Lippincott Company, 1979.

Keddie, Kenneth M.G. "Pathological Mourning after the Death of a Domestic Pet." *Brit. J. Psychiat.*, vol. 131 (1977), pp. 21–5.

Kirk, Robert Warren. *First Aid for Pets.* New York: Dutton, 1978.

Kübler-Ross, Elisabeth. *On Death and Dying.* New York: Macmillan. 1973.

Levinson, Boris M. *Pets and Human Development.* Springfield, Ill.: Chas. C. Thomas, 1972.

Lorenz, Konrad. Z. *King Solomon's Ring.* London: Methuen, 1952.

Madden, Murdaugh Stuart. "Arrangements for Pets in Your Will." *Humane Society News*, Fall 1978.

Newman, Steven A. "Pet Peeves." *New York*, March 1979.

Nieburg, Herbert A. "Pathological Grief in Response to Loss of Domestic Pets." *DVM*, Feb. 1979.

———. "Pet Loss: Helping Owners Cope." *DVM*, March 1979.

Parkes, Colin Murray. *Bereavement: Studies of Grief in Adult Life.* New York: International Universities Press, 1974.

Perry, Eleanor. "Hail and Farewell: An Epitaph for Lulu." *New York Times*, June 28, 1978.

Pugnetti, Gino. *Simon and Schuster's Guide to Dogs.* New York: Simon and Schuster, 1980.

"Report of the American Veterinary Medical Association Panel on Euthanasia." *J.A.V.M.A.*, vol. 173, no. 1 (1978), pp. 59–72.

Rynearson, E.K. "Humans and Pets and Attachment." *Brit. J. Psychiat.*, vol. 133 (1978), pp. 550–55.

Symposium on Pet Loss and Human Emotion. New York, 1981.

Tatelbaum, Judy. *The Courage to Grieve.* New York: Lippincott and Crowell, 1980.

Wax, Judith A. "A Death in the Family." *New York Times*, April 22, 1979.

Weisman, Avery D. *On Dying and Denying: A Psychiatric Study of Terminality.* New York: Behavioral Publications, 1972.

Wilbourn, Carole C. *The Inner Cat: A New Approach to Cat Behavior.* New York: Stein and Day, 1978.

Worden, J. William, and William Proctor. *PDA—Personal Death Awareness.* Englewood Cliffs: Prentice-Hall, 1976.

Wright, Phyllis, "Why Must We Euthanize?" *The Humane Society News*, Summer 1978.

———. "To Find a Good Home." *The Humane Society News*, Spring 1980.

Index